First World War
and Army of Occupation
War Diary
France, Belgium and Germany

24 DIVISION
Divisional Troops
Divisional Trench Mortar Batteries
6 January 1916 - 24 February 1919

WO95/2198/2

The Naval & Military Press Ltd
www.nmarchive.com
Published in association with The National Archives

Published by

The Naval & Military Press Ltd

Unit 10 Ridgewood Industrial Park,

Uckfield, East Sussex,

TN22 5QE England

Tel: +44 (0) 1825 749494

www.naval-military-press.com

www.nmarchive.com

This diary has been reprinted in facsimile from the original. Any imperfections are inevitably reproduced and the quality may fall short of modern type and cartographic standards.

© **Crown Copyright**
Images reproduced by permission of The National Archives, London, England, 2015.

Contents

Document type	Place/Title	Date From	Date To
Heading	WO95/2198/2 Divisional Trench Mortar Batteries		
Heading	24th Division Divl Artillery Divl Trench Mortar Bttys Jan 1916-Jan 1919		
Heading	20 Trench Motar Btn Jan Vol III		
War Diary		06/01/1916	31/01/1916
Heading	To D.A.G. 3rd Echelon	01/09/1916	01/09/1916
War Diary		01/07/1916	31/07/1916
War Diary		01/08/1916	31/08/1916
War Diary		01/09/1916	13/09/1916
War Diary		01/10/1916	31/10/1916
War Diary		01/09/1916	30/09/1916
War Diary	Carnoy	01/09/1916	06/09/1916
War Diary	Bois de Tailles	07/09/1916	11/09/1916
War Diary	Carnoy	13/09/1916	28/09/1916
War Diary	Bois de Tailles	29/09/1916	30/09/1916
War Diary	Carnoy	01/09/1916	07/09/1916
War Diary	Bois des Tailles	08/09/1916	10/09/1916
War Diary	Carnoy	11/09/1916	27/09/1916
War Diary	Bois des Tailles	28/09/1916	29/09/1916
War Diary	Amiens	30/09/1916	30/09/1916
War Diary	Bruay	01/10/1916	03/10/1916
War Diary	Vimy	04/10/1916	31/10/1916
War Diary	Barry	01/10/1916	02/10/1916
War Diary	Camblain L'abbe	03/10/1916	03/10/1916
War Diary	Vimy Ridge	04/10/1916	18/10/1916
War Diary	Vimy	19/10/1916	31/10/1916
War Diary	Barry	01/10/1916	01/10/1916
War Diary	Camblain L'abbe	02/10/1916	03/10/1916
War Diary	Vimy Ridge	04/10/1916	31/10/1916
War Diary	Vimy	01/11/1916	30/11/1916
War Diary	Vimy Ridge	01/11/1916	30/11/1916
Heading	From Browne Bill Nominal Rolls of 2		
War Diary	Vinny	01/10/1916	03/10/1916
War Diary	Loos	04/10/1916	31/10/1916
War Diary	Vinny	01/12/1916	03/12/1916
War Diary	Vinny	04/12/1916	31/12/1916
Miscellaneous	18th Army Field Artillery Brigade		
War Diary	Divisional Ammunition Column.	25/12/1916	25/12/1916
War Diary	Hulluch	01/01/1917	31/01/1917
War Diary	Map 36'c N. 25 d 88 Loos	01/01/1917	31/01/1917
War Diary	Head Qrs Houchin Map 36B	01/02/1917	03/02/1917
War Diary	Head Qrs Houchin	04/02/1917	08/02/1917
War Diary	Head Qrs	09/02/1917	13/02/1917
War Diary	Hd Qrs Bourecq Map 36A	14/02/1917	18/02/1917
War Diary	Head Qrs Manque Ville Map 36 A	19/02/1917	21/02/1917
War Diary	Head Qrs Manque Ville	23/02/1917	28/02/1917
War Diary	Hulloch	01/02/1917	13/02/1917
War Diary	Lespesse	14/02/1917	18/02/1917
War Diary	Ham En Artois	18/02/1917	28/02/1917
War Diary	Loos	01/02/1917	13/02/1917

War Diary	Les Brebis	14/02/1917	14/02/1917
War Diary	Lespesse	18/02/1917	18/02/1917
War Diary	Head Qrs Manque Ville	01/03/1917	04/03/1917
War Diary	Head Qrs Houchin	05/03/1917	08/03/1917
War Diary	Hd Qrs Houchin Map 36 B	09/03/1917	31/03/1917
War Diary	Calonne	09/03/1917	31/03/1917
War Diary	Angus	07/03/1917	31/03/1917
War Diary	Hezecques	01/05/1917	01/05/1917
War Diary	Oudezeele	10/05/1917	10/05/1917
War Diary	Halifax Camp	18/05/1917	18/05/1917
War Diary	Hill 60 Sector	24/05/1917	31/05/1917
Heading	Trench Mortar Batteries 24th Division April 1917		
War Diary	Couchy	01/04/1917	24/04/1917
War Diary	Calonne	01/04/1917	23/04/1917
War Diary	Hezecques	24/04/1917	24/04/1917
War Diary	Angres Scts	01/04/1917	13/04/1917
War Diary	Cite Calonne	14/04/1917	30/04/1917
War Diary	Hezecques.	01/05/1917	09/05/1917
War Diary	Hazebrouck	10/05/1917	10/05/1917
War Diary	Oudezeel	11/05/1917	11/05/1917
War Diary	Zillebeke	24/05/1917	31/05/1917
War Diary	Hill 60	25/05/1917	31/05/1917
War Diary	Ypres	01/06/1917	30/06/1917
War Diary	Ypres	01/07/1917	04/07/1917
War Diary	Racquinghem	05/07/1917	14/07/1917
War Diary	Ypres	15/07/1917	24/07/1917
War Diary	Ypres	25/07/1917	31/07/1917
War Diary	Ypres	01/08/1917	31/08/1917
Miscellaneous	24 Div T.M. Battalion Vol 15 Sep 1917		
War Diary	Ypres	01/09/1917	14/09/1917
War Diary	Steenvoorde	15/09/1917	17/09/1917
War Diary	Bapaume	18/09/1917	24/09/1917
War Diary	Doingt	25/09/1917	28/09/1917
War Diary	Hervilly	29/09/1917	30/09/1917
Heading	War Diary For Month Of October 1917 Of 24th D.T.M.O. Vol 16		
War Diary	Hervilly	01/10/1917	31/10/1917
Heading	War Diary 24th Divisional Trench Mortar Batteries From Nov 1st To Nov 30th 1917 Vol 17		
War Diary	Hervilly	01/11/1917	29/11/1917
Heading	24th Divisional Trench Mortar Batteries War Diary For The Month December 1917 Vol 18		
War Diary	Hargicourt.	01/12/1917	31/12/1917
War Diary	Loos	01/01/1917	13/02/1917
War Diary	Lespesse	14/02/1917	18/02/1917
War Diary	Ham. En. Artois	28/02/1917	28/02/1917
War Diary		12/03/1917	31/03/1917
War Diary	Hezecques	01/05/1917	01/05/1917
War Diary	Oudezeele	10/05/1917	10/05/1917
War Diary	Halifax Camp	18/05/1917	18/05/1917
War Diary	Hill 60	25/05/1917	31/05/1917
Heading	24th Divisional Trench Mortar Batteries War Diary for the month of January 1918. Vol 19		
War Diary	Hargicourt	01/01/1918	31/01/1918
Heading	War Diary Month of February 1918 24th Divisional Trench Mortar Battery		

War Diary	Hargicourt	01/02/1918	05/03/1918
War Diary	Beaumetz	06/03/1918	12/03/1918
War Diary	Le Verguier	13/03/1918	31/03/1918
Heading	War Diary 24th Divisional Trench Mortar Batteries, April 1918		
Heading	24th Divisional F M Batteries War Diary for month of April 1918 Vol 22		
War Diary	Rumingy	01/04/1918	02/04/1918
War Diary	Cottenchy	03/04/1918	07/04/1918
War Diary	Dury	09/08/1918	09/08/1918
War Diary	Clairy	10/08/1918	10/08/1918
War Diary	Andainville	11/08/1918	12/08/1918
War Diary	Wanel	13/08/1918	17/08/1918
War Diary	Wavans	18/08/1918	18/08/1918
War Diary	Ramecourt	19/08/1918	21/08/1918
War Diary	Berlencourt	22/08/1918	30/08/1918
Heading	24th Divisional Trench Mortar Batteries Vol 23 War Diary for the month of May 1918. Vol 23		
War Diary	Berlencourt	01/05/1918	02/05/1918
War Diary	Lens	03/05/1918	31/05/1918
Heading	War Diary of Divisional Trench mortar officer 24th Div. Artillery From 1st June 1918 to 30th June 1918. Vol 24		
War Diary	Field	01/06/1918	30/06/1918
Heading	War Diary of 24th. Divisional Trench Mortar Officer. From 1st July, 1918 To 31st July 1918. Vol 25		
War Diary	Field	01/07/1918	31/07/1918
Heading	War Diary of 2 Divisional Trench Mortar Officer. (24th Division). Vol 26		
War Diary	Field	01/08/1918	31/12/1918
War Diary	Chercq	01/01/1919	24/02/1919

WO/95/2198/2
Divisional Trench Mortar
Batteries

24TH DIVISION
DIVL ARTILLERY

DIVL TRENCH MORTAR BTTYS
JAN 1916 - JAN 1919.

2.0 Trench Mortar Bty 24
Jan
Vol VII

Jan '16
July '16
Jan '19

20th Trench Mortar Bty

WAR DIARY
or
INTELLIGENCE SUMMARY
(Erase heading not required.)

Army Form C. 2118

Instructions regarding War Diaries and Intelligence Summaries are contained in F.S. Regs., Part II. and the Staff Manual respectively. Title Pages will be prepared in manuscript.

Place	Date	Hour	Summary of Events and Information	Remarks and references to Appendices
	6-1-16		Brought 1 N.C.O. & 4 men up into trenches & took over from Lieut Higgins at 6 a.m.	
	7-1-16		Took an inventory of stores handed over by 27th T.M.B.S. Was shown round gun emplacements etc. There was only two beds in action. One 2" & one 1½" position having been blown in by shell fire. There was considerable artillery activity on both sides during the day. On 12.30 am the enemy opened fire with machine guns. Only four 120 lb bombs were sent over. No firing. Lieut Higgins left at 5 p.m. for rest camp. Lieut Aplin joined me at 6.30 a.m. Some orders for sand bags to be used for strengthening both mens dug-outs.	
	8-1-16		Heavy Artillery fire directed on our trenches by enemy. Had the beds in the Cater hauled out. No firing. Wired for Ammunition. Twenty rounds of 1½" Ammunition arrived. The men continued strengthening dug-outs after dark. Visited by Lieut Vale.	
	9-1-16		Heavily shelled by guns & Trench Mortars. Retaliated by firing four 33U bombs. The enemy sent over eight 120 lb bombs during the day.	
	10-1-16		Everything quiet no firing. Am being relieved by Lieut Vale tonight. Left the trenches at 5 p.m.	

Army Form C. 2118

WAR DIARY
or
INTELLIGENCE SUMMARY
(Erase heading not required.)

Instructions regarding War Diaries and Intelligence Summaries are contained in F.S. Regs., Part II. and the Staff Manual respectively. Title Pages will be prepared in manuscript.

Place	Date	Hour	Summary of Events and Information	Remarks and references to Appendices
	10-1-16		Took over from Lr Clayton. Normal	
	11-1-16		Went round area & chose position	
	12-1-16		One 12" & One 2" placed in action	
	13-1-16		Normal.	
	14-1-16		One 12" gun placed in action	
	15-1-16		Handed over to Lieut Clayton	
	15-1-16		Relieved Lieut Vale at 6 p.m.	
	16-1-16		Fired 8.60 pounders and 10 pounders from 1½" gun at point 01 (Fop Head) Enemy retaliated with Minenwerfers. One direct hit on 2" Bed completely destroyed it. Seven 120 pound bombs in all were sent over. French leading to dug-out badly blown in in three places Reported loss to O.C. T.M. Batteries	
	17-1-16		No firing Everything quiet Considerable Artillery activity during afternoon. Men working until 2 a.m. getting trench straight. 10 2 inch & 10 1½ inch ammunition received	
	18-1-16		8 thirty three pounders and 5 By Lt Fired at Snipers post completely destroyed. Enemy searched for guns with 4.2 & Whizz-bangs. Received new 2nd feel & 20 rounds of 15 said Ammunition	
	19-1-16		5 thirty three pounders fired at snipers post situated to the left of the last one. Enemy retaliated with shell fire No damage done	
	20-1-16		Took over from Lieut Clayton	
	21-1-16		At 2.30 p.m. opened fire at enemys front line to register got into 18th in their front line Both burst No retaliation yet.	

Army Form C. 2118

WAR DIARY
or
INTELLIGENCE SUMMARY
(Erase heading not required.)

Instructions regarding War Diaries and Intelligence Summaries are contained in F.S. Regs., Part II. and the Staff Manual respectively. Title Pages will be prepared in manuscript.

Place	Date	Hour	Summary of Events and Information	Remarks and references to Appendices
	22-1-16		Spent night making trench to lead to dug-out	
	23-1-16		Fired at 9.30 – 4 12" at their front line all burst just in or out. At 4.5" fired one 33ᵃ in their line burst. Corporal Cox wounded by fragment of 9.2 shell	
	24-1-16		Normal. Heavy shelling by Huns in morning.	
	25-1-16		Relieved Lieut Vale at 7.30 pm. Bombt Harry shot through the head by machine gun bullet as we were coming up the Menin Road. Heavily shelled with whizz bangs at midnight. 9.2am fired down 12" bombs at enemys second line opposite C4. Enemy retaliated with a few whizz bangs & rifle grenades. Received a visit from O.C. T.M. 8ᵗʰ Bgᵉ Fired 5 heavy 12" bomb at snipers post opposite C.4. Result satisfactory. No retaliation. Visited by Lieuts Asprey & Vale	
	26-1-16		New 12" gun emplacement also 3.7 emplacement made in C.S.S. last night. Fired 5" heavy 12" in bombs at German support line where there were some deep'ents. Considerable damage was done in the neighbourhood of hostile. Enemy retaliated with rifle grenades. Visited by O.C. T.M. B 8ᵗʰ (in Capt) The two 12" in gun positions having jumped were moved last night. Fired 4 light 15" bombs at enemys fire trench opposite C.4. The Huns were heard to blow three flasks on a whistle and to yell out "look out". Enemy retaliated with whizz bangs & rifle grenades	
	28-1-16		New gun emplacement made in Crater to 9.7 last night. Fired 5 heavy 12" bombs at daybreak on Huns fire trenches to the left of stables. Two bombs didn't arrive, were considerable damage to trench. The other bursts were also satisfactory. No retaliation damage to parapet a trifle with whizz bangs & heavy shell from Heavily bombarded for three quarters of an hour	
	30-1-16		Hill 60. Four tried hits on dug-out. Fired 2 heavy 15" bombs at snipers post opposite C.5. difficult to observe on account of heavy mist. Sergt Scott Section relieved by Sgt Haneys.	

1875 (W. W593/826 1,000,000 4/15 J.B.C. & A. A.D.S.S./Forms/C. 2118.

WAR DIARY
or
INTELLIGENCE SUMMARY

Army Form C. 2118

(Erase heading not required.)

Place	Date	Hour	Summary of Events and Information	Remarks and references to Appendices
	3/4/16		New 9.7 emplacement made by signallers dug out last night. Trench gun again strengthened in Crater. No firing to-day. Relieved by Lieut Vale.	

P C Clayton "Lieut R.F.A.
for O.C. 20 "French Mortar Battery
24 Division

To: D.A.G. 3rd Echelon TM 4 24

Herewith War Diaries for July 1916.
I regret these are on ordinary paper, but we have run out of War Diary forms, & are unable to obtain any from neighbouring units.
These forms are on indent, but have not yet arrived.

1.9.16.

E.H. Cumming Capt.
O.C. T.M. Batty
24th D.A.

July 1916. WAR DIARY X AND Z. T.M. B's

1st July	X, and Z. Not Engaged.
2nd "	X, Not Engaged.
	Z. Fired 2 Rd. in Retaliation to Enemies Trench Mortars.
3rd "	⎫
4th "	⎬ Not Engaged.
5th "	⎭
6th "	During Arty. Bombardment. X, Fired 17, and Z, 37 Rds. At Enemies Front Line and Supports.
7th "	⎫
8th "	⎬ Australian Relief Takes Place.
9th "	⎭
10th "	⎫
11th "	⎬ X AND Z. Completed 4 new gun positions and Bomb Stores.
12th "	X. Fired 4 Rds. in Retaliation.
	Z. Not Engaged.
13th "	X. Fired 1 Rd.
	Z. Not Engaged.
14th "	⎫
15th "	⎬ X AND Z. Not Engaged.
16th "	X. Fired 10 Rds. Z. Fired 15 Rds. in Retaliation to Enemies Trench Mortars.
17th "	X. AND Z. Not Engaged.

18th July	During Arty. Bombardment X Fired 16 Rds. Z Fired 14 Rds at enemies front line and supports.
19th "	X and Z not engaged.
20th "	X not engaged. Z Fired 12 Rds. in retaliation.
21st "	X not engaged. Z Fired 8 Rds. in retaliation.
21st/22 "	Relieved by 31th Div. T.M.B's
23rd to 31st "	On the move.

L. B. Huggins 2nd Lt.
O.C X/24 T.M. 13

War Diary for the month of July.

1st
8.30 p.m.   Fired 9 rounds on enemy's front line trench in retaliation for enemy's trench mortars, on Petite Douve Farm.

2nd
10.30 p.m.   Fired 24 rounds, on Ash Road Barrier also enemy's front line trench Petite Douve Farm.

3rd
Not engaged.

4th
Not engaged.
Started building new gun emplacement in support trench.

5th
Not engaged.
Finished gun emplacement in support trench.
Started to build bomb store.
2 Lieut A.A. Emmett. R.F.A. joined for duty.

6th
Took part in Artillery Strafe.
Fired 51 rounds at enemy's front line trench on Ash Road Barrier and Petite Douve Farm
Finished Bomb store.

7th — Relieved by the French Mortar Batteries of the 41st Division.

8th — Not engaged. Proceeded to Locre.

9th — Returned from Locre.
Battery moved to another position at N.29.D. took over from X/50. French Mortar Battery two gun emplacements and 20 rounds of ammunition
2/Lieut. C.A. McMurtry R.F.A. proceeded to join A/107.

10th — Not engaged.

11th — Not engaged.
Rebedded emplacements and strengthened roofing
Dug small communication trench.

12th — Not engaged.

13th — Fired 4 rounds for registration purposes and dug sump to drain bomb store & emplacement.

14th — Not engaged.
Cleaned guns &stores.

15th   Not engaged. Building new gun position

16th   Not engaged.
Built Bomb store and drained old emplacement.

17th   Not engaged.
10 new gun positions selected.

18th   Not engaged.
Started to build new gun emplacement and strengthened old emplacement.

19th   Not engaged.

20th   Not engaged.

21st   Not engaged.

22nd   Handed over to the Trench Mortar Batteries 36th Division.

23rd   Battery went out of action into Rest billets

24th to 31st   Rest Billets.

C.D.B. Swain Lieut. R.F.A.
O.C. Y.24. Trench Mortar Battery.

1/9/16.

Heavy M
T M Batts
Vol 2

War Diary for the month of August.

1st   Rest billets. Vecquemont.

2nd   Rest billets. Vecquemont.

3rd   Rest billets. Vecquemont.

4th   Battery move into rest billets at the "Bois de Tailles".

5th   Rest billets. Bois de Tailles.

6th   Rest billets. Bois de Tailles.

7th   Rest billets. Bois de Tailles.

8th   Started to dig gun pits for D/107. Brigade. R.F.A. but were recalled at midnight, as they were not required.

9th   Rest billets. Bois de Tailles.

10th   A party of men from the battery proceeded by lorry to Carnoy to dig gun pits and dug outs for the 106th Brigade. R.F.A.

11th   Battery moved to Carnoy and took over billets from the 2nd Division Trench Mortar Batteries.

12th   A party of men from the Battery under one officer were sent up to continue the work, for D/106. Brigade. R.F.A.

13th — Went up to the trenches with Capt. Fanning. M.C. to select battery position.

14th — Battery went into Action.
Selected one gun position, and started work on same.

15th — Finished gun emplacement about stores, and brought up ammunition.

16th — Fired 37 rounds on enemy's strong point.

17th — Cleaned gun stores.

18th — Not engaged.

19th — Not engaged.

20th — Not engaged.

21st — Our infantry made an attack and succeeded in taking Guillemont Station.

22nd — Not engaged.

23rd — Not engaged.
Cleaned gun stores.

24th   Not engaged.

25th   Not engaged.

26th   Not engaged.

27th   Not engaged.

28th   Not engaged.
        Cleaned gun & stores.

29th   Not engaged.

30th   Not engaged.

31st   Not engaged.
        Cleaned gun & stores also ammunition.

31/8/16   C.G. Higgins 2nd LT
                        O.C X/24 T.M.B.

War Diary for the month of August.

1st	Rest billets. Vecquemont.
2nd	Rest billets. Vecquemont.
3rd	Rest billets. Vecquemont.
4th	Battery move into rest billets at the "Bois de Tailles".
5th	Rest billets. Bois de Tailles.
6th	Rest billets. Bois de Tailles.
7th	Rest billets. Bois de Tailles.
8th	Battery started to dig gun pits for D/107 Brigade R.F.A. but were recalled at 2 a.m., as they were not required.
9th	Rest billets. Bois de Tailles.
10th	A party of men from the battery proceeded by Lorry to Carnoy to dig gun pits and dug outs for the 106th Brigade R.F.A.
11th	Battery moved to Carnoy and took over billets from the 2nd Division Trench Mortar Batteries.
12th	A party of men from the battery under one officer were sent off to continue the work for the 106th Brigade R.F.A. Went up to the trenches with Capt. Fanning. M.C. to

Select battery position.

13th — Battery went into action near Waterlot Farm to engage the T. trench.

14th — Selected four gun positions, and started to dig gun emplacements.

15th — Finished two gun emplacements and bomb stores.

16th — Started work on remaining two gun emplacements

17th — Finished two gun emplacements also bomb stores. Brought up ammunition.

18th — Ordered to put in two more gun emplacements.

19th — Selected two gun positions & started work on them.

20th — Finished building gun emplacements and bomb stores.
Carried round ammunition.

21st — Our infantry made an attack and succeeded in taking Guillemont Station.

22nd — Rebuilt one gun emplacement which had been blown in during yesterday's bombardment.

23rd — Battery ordered out of action.

24th — Battery ordered to take up a position in Pioneer trench to engage a strong point.

Selected two gun positions.
Two guns & stores taken up to trenches.

25th Started building two gun emplacements.

26th Finished building two gun emplacements and bomb stores.
Brought ammunition round from old emplacements.

27th Cleaned guns & stores also ammunition.

28th Gun positions flooded out owing to bad weather, decided to build two new gun emplacements a little further down the trench.

29th Selected two gun positions.

30th Started to build two gun emplacements

31st Gun emplacements & bomb stores nearly completed.

A.D. Swain Lieut R.G.A.
O.C. Y.24. Trench Mortar Battery

31/8/16.

War Diary. Aug^st 1916.

1st — Rest Billets. Vecquemont.

2nd — Rest Billets. Vecquemont.

3rd — Rest Billets. Vecquemont.

4th — Battery moves up to Reserve Area "Bois de Tailles".

5th — In bivouac. Bois de Tailles.

6th — In bivouac. Bois de Tailles.

7th — In bivouac. Bois de Tailles.

8th — Battery detailed to dig gun pits for D/107 Bgde. R.F.A. Battery recalled at 2 a.m. Gun pits not required.

9th — In bivouac. Bois de Tailles.

10th — Party from battery proceed to CARNOY by lorry, to dig gun pits & dug-outs for 106th Bgde R.F.A. Returned to Bois de Tailles 7.30 p.m.

11th — Battery moved to CARNOY. Took over billets from T.M. Battery 2nd D.A.

12th — Battery continued digging for 106th Bgde R.F.A.

13th — Not in action.

14th — Carried ammunition for Y battery.

15th   Carried ammunition for 'Y' battery.

16th   Not in action

17th   Relieve 'X' battery in ~~scout~~ position opp SUNKEN ROAD. (S.30.d 6½. 7½ Trench Map GUILLEMONT).

18th   ~~Not Engaged~~ Not Engaged.

19th   Not Engaged. Improve gun pits

20th   Not Engaged. Make further ammunition recesses. Laid out new lines of fire on German S.P.

21st   Not Engaged. Guillemont Stn taken by our infantry.

22nd   Relieved by 'X' battery in morning. Made splinter proofs for A/109 Bgde RFA on left of BERNAFAY WOOD

~~23rd~~

23rd   Not in Action.

24th   Dug Gun pits for 'X' battery.

25th   In conjunction with 'X' battery took 4 gg more guns into action at (S 24 d. 4½. ½. Ref GUILLEMONT Trench Map).

26th   Carried ammunition for X battery.

27th   Took over position (S 30.d. 6½. 7½ Ref GUILLEMONT Trench Map) from 'X' battery.

28th   Not engaged.

29th   Not Engaged.

30th   Not Engaged. Weather very bad. Heavy rains.

31st   Not Engaged. Rain continues. Very difficult to
        drain gun pits.
        Ammunition, 30 per, day.

                                L. S. Davis 2/Lt.
                                O. C. Z. Battery
                                T. M. Arty
                                24th Division

X/24 T.M.B. Army Form C. 2118.

WAR DIARY FOR SEPTEMBER 1916
OR INTELLIGENCE SUMMARY
(Erase heading not required.)

Place	Date	Hour	Summary of Events and Information	Remarks and references to Appendices
	1st		Repaired gun positions in SAPPER TRENCH.	
	2nd		Working party bomb carrying.	
	3rd		During attack on GUILLEMONT and GINCHY X Battery fired 34 Rds, 10 L dug-out, 9 at man in ORCHARD and 15 at BARRIER on SUNKEN ROAD.	
	4th		Not Engaged.	
	5th		Came out of action.	
	6th		Relieved by GUARDS Div. Moved from CARNOY to BOIS du TAILLES.	
	7th		Resting.	
	8th		Cleaning guns and stores.	
	9th		Fatigue.	
	10th		Gun drill.	
	11th		Returned to CARNOY.	
	12th		Working party for 106 Bde.	
	13th		Working party for 109 Bde.	
	14th		Working party for 109 Bde.	
	15th		Resting.	
	16th		Kit Inspection and fatigue.	

Army Form C. 2118.

WAR DIARY
or
INTELLIGENCE SUMMARY
(Erase heading not required.)

Instructions regarding War Diaries and Intelligence Summaries are contained in F. S. Regs., Part II. and the Staff Manual respectively. Title Pages will be prepared in manuscript.

Place	Date	Hour	Summary of Events and Information	Remarks and references to Appendices
	17th		Gun drill and fatigues	
	18th		Working party, road making 10 & Bde.	
	19th		Working party, Battery fatigues 10 & ...	
	20th		" " road making 10 & ...	
	21st		Y.ctrgun	
	22nd		Working party 10 & Bde.	
	23rd		Kit inspection	
	24th		Gun drill, inspection and fatigues	
	25th		Six men go into action with Y Battery	
	26th		Carrying party for Battery in action	
	27th		Working party Road making	
	28th		Relieved by 4 Div T.M.B. returned to Bois du Tailles	
	29th		Resting	
	30th		Entrained for BRUAY.	

S.G. Higgins Lt
OC 7/24 T.M.B.

WAR DIARY
or
INTELLIGENCE SUMMARY

(Erase heading not required.)

Army Form C. 2118.

X 24 T.M. Bty
Div T.M. Batts
Vol. 3

Place	Date	Hour	Summary of Events and Information	Remarks and references to Appendices
Trony Sept	1		Limbered two Gun trips with shrub stove: components, ammunition for that position	
	2		20 two Bombs sent up to Gun Craters	
	3		Battery fired 20 Gun bombs and 5 H.E. into Emplacement	
	4		Proceeded to trenches to reconnoitre three Gun Craters in Emplacement	
	5		Dug three gun positions and three trench store	
	6		Battery ordered into action & away been relieved by 23rd Div T.Hs. and proceeded to Ross Bellis at Piove di Sallie	
Pin di Sallie	7		at Piove di Sallies in Rest	
	8		" "	
	9		" "	
	10		Received orders to move to Barony	
	11			
	12		Proceeded to Barony by lorries	
Barony	13		Erected experimental entrenchments for 10 6.T.A.B.	
	14		Working party again provided for 10 6.T.A.B. "	
	15		In Rest	
	16		"	
	17		"	
	18		Working party provided for 106. T. A.B.	
	19		" " 109th " "	
	20		" " 108th " "	
	21		" " 107th " "	

Army Form C. 2118.

WAR DIARY
or
INTELLIGENCE SUMMARY

(Erase heading not required.)

Instructions regarding War Diaries and Intelligence Summaries are contained in F. S. Regs., Part II. and the Staff Manual respectively. Title Pages will be prepared in manuscript.

Place	Date	Hour	Summary of Events and Information	Remarks and references to Appendices
Bovary Ridge	23		Resting	
	24		"	
	25		Battn. moved forward before attack on Leo Bouf to go into action if required	
	26		Occupied forward position but not being required to go into action returned in the evening to Cannon	
	27		Resting – received orders to move	
	28		Move to Bois de Tailles	
Bois de Tailles	29		Resting	
	30		Proceeded by motor lorries to Mericourt to entrain for Picardy	

C.H. Moran Lieut. Agr.
O.C. Y 24. Trench Mortar Battery

30/9/16.

Army Form C. 2118.

2/24 T. M. B.

WAR DIARY
or
INTELLIGENCE SUMMARY

(Erase heading not required.)

Instructions regarding War Diaries and Intelligence Summaries are contained in F. S. Regs., Part II. and the Staff Manual respectively. Title Pages will be prepared in manuscript.

Place	Date	Hour	Summary of Events and Information	Remarks and references to Appendices
Barmy	1/9/16	6 p.m.	Not Engaged, at Rest Billets.	
do.	2/9/16	do.	March & carrying party for Y Battery up to Vivier. French offered gentlemen	
			Station under fire is a 48 gun emplacement. 20 gas bombs are taken up by this party.	
do.	3/9/16	9 p.m.	Not Engaged at Rest Billets.	
do.	4/9/16	do.	Take a party up at dawn to get Trench stores together & batteries in reserve French	
do.	5/9/16	do.	We are relieved by the French Division. 8th Army de Fouille & Sept.	
do.	6/9/16	do.		
Bois des Fouilles	7/9/16	do.	Not Engaged, at Rest	
do.	8/9/16	do.	do.	
do.	9/9/16	do.	do.	
do.	10/9/16	do.	do.	
do.	11/9/16	do.	Leave Bois de Fouilles & return to Barmy, when one killed in an orchard in this Coy.	
Barmy	11/9/16	do.	Leave Bois de Fouilles & return to Barmy.	
			The road leads to Montauban.	
do.	12/9/16	do.	Not Engaged at Rest Billets	
do.	13/9/16	do.	Provide a working party for 103 P.I. G.O. under command of T.L. Higgins 1/24 T.M.B.	
do.	14/9/16	do.	Continue yesterday's work Grand building from which wood to gentlemen under	
			Command of Lt. H. Davis 2/24 T.M.B.	
do.	15/9/16	do.	Not Engaged at Rest Billets.	
do.	16/9/16	do.	do.	
do.	17/9/16	do.	do.	

Army Form C. 2118.

WAR DIARY
or
INTELLIGENCE SUMMARY

(Erase heading not required.)

Z/2 ..... T.M.B.

Place	Date	Hour	Summary of Events and Information	Remarks and references to Appendices
Barov	18/9/16	6 p.m	Provide a working party for 106th T.M.B. under command of 2/Lt. Emmott to 1/24 T.M.B.	
do.	19/9/16	do.	Working party for 109th T.M.B. under Lt. Swan 1/24 T.M.B.	
do.	20/9/16	do.	" 108th T.M.B. " 2/Lt. Ramsay 1/24 T.M.B.	
do.	21/9/16	do.	" 109th T.M.B. " 2/Lt. Emmott 1/24 T.M.B.	
do.	22/9/16	do.	Not engaged at Red Billets.	
do.	23/9/16	do.	do.	
do.	24/9/16	do.	do.	
do.	25/9/16	do.	Go up with a section of T.M. Bty. & 50 sols. to Gueudecourt, when we remain in reserve to 16th & 18th B.F. 96 in case required.	
do.	26/9/16	do.	Not having been required, we return to Billets at midday.	
do.	27/9/16	do.	Not engaged at Red Billets.	
Bois des Tailles	28/9/16	do.	We are relieved by the 4th Division.	
do.	29/9/16	do.	Not engaged. Resting.	
do.	30/9/16	do.	We proceed to Bienvillers l'Abbaye by lorry & entrain for Bruay, & detrain this night en route for this new area	

Army Form C. 2118.

WAR DIARY or INTELLIGENCE SUMMARY

(Erase heading not required.)

For OCT. 1916   X/24 T.M.B.

Vol 4   24

Instructions regarding War Diaries and Intelligence Summaries are contained in F. S. Regs., Part II. and the Staff Manual respectively. Title Pages will be prepared in manuscript.

Place	Date	Hour	Summary of Events and Information	Remarks and references to Appendices
Bruay	1st	6 pm	Arrived (Bruay)	
	2nd	7 am	Left Bruay for Comblain L'Abbé	
	3rd	5 pm	Reconnoitred new positions on Vimy Ridge	
Vimy	4th	11 am	Relieved X/19 T.M.B.	
	5th	10 am	Registered No 4 Gun.	
	6th	8 am	Fired 10 rds into craters — observed.	
		12.15 pm	Fired 10 rds at front line S.15.C.5.4½	
		2.30 pm	Fired 20 rds 100 t [?] boiler	
		11.30 pm	Fired 10 rds into craters on reliefshot [?]	
			Relieved No 4 gun Bed.	
	7th	7.30 am	Fired 10 rds into Crater No 9 and 17	
		11 am	Fired 5 rds at front line S.15.C.3½.5	
		11.15 am	Fired 10 rds into Crater No 17.	
		12.45 pm	Fired 10 rds into Crater mortalaters [?]	
		2.40 pm	Fired 5 rds S.15.C.5.4½	
			Relieved No 1 Gun Bed	
	8th	7.30 am	Fired 10 rds into Crater No 9 and 17	
		11.30 am	Fired 10 rds at front line S.15.C.5.4½	

Army Form C. 2118.

N2H T.M.B

WAR DIARY
or
INTELLIGENCE SUMMARY

(Erase heading not required.)

Instructions regarding War Diaries and Intelligence Summaries are contained in F. S. Regs., Part II. and the Staff Manual respectively. Title Pages will be prepared in manuscript.

Place	Date	Hour	Summary of Events and Information	Remarks and references to Appendices
	8th	7.40 p.m	Fired 10 rds into Crater S.15.C.9.9.	
		3.45 p.m	Fired 10 rds at S.15.C.4.5	
			About front of No 3 gun position which had fallen in	
	9th	8 a.m	Fired 10 rds into Crater 35 S.15.A.6.0	
		11.30 am	Fired 10 rds into Crater 17 S.15.C.9.9.	
		1.15 pm	Fired 10 rds at front S.15.C.8.8	
		2.30 pm	Fired 10 rds S.15.D.0.8.	
	10th	7 a.m	Fired 20 rds at points S.15.C.9.9. and S.15.A.6.0.	
		1.30 pm	Fired 10 rds at point S.15.C.3.5.	
		3.15 pm	Fired 10 rds at points S.15.C.5.4.	
	11th	7.45 am	Fired 5 rds at Lady Group	
		8 a.m	Fired 5 rds at S.15.C.5.5.	
		9.45 am	Fired 10 rds at point S.15.C.35 new relations	
		1.20 pm	Fired 10 rds strafe S.15.C.9.8.	
		3 p.m	Fired 10 rds strafe S.15.D.1.8.	
		4.45 pm	Fired 15 retaliation {5 rds 15.C.4.5 / 10 rds 15.D.1.8.	
	12th	11 a.m	Fired 8 rds S.15.C.5.4. strafe.	
		2.30 pm	Fired 25 rds S.15.D.1.8. strafe.	

Army Form C. 2118.

X/24 1 M.B

WAR DIARY
or
INTELLIGENCE SUMMARY
(Erase heading not required.)

Instructions regarding War Diaries and Intelligence Summaries are contained in F. S. Regs., Part II and the Staff Manual respectively. Title Pages will be prepared in manuscript.

Place	Date	Hour	Summary of Events and Information	Remarks and references to Appendices
	13th	9 a.m.	Fired 10 rds S.15.D.18. strafe	
		10.30 a.m.	Fired 21 rds S.15.C.5.4. strafe	
		3 p.m.	Fired 20 rds S.15.D.1.8. strafe	
		3.30 p.m.	Fired 5 rds S.15.C.5.4. strafe	
	14th	9 a.m.	Fired 10 rds S.15.D.1.8. strafe	
		10.45 a.m.	Fired 17 rds S.15.C.4.5. strafe	
		3.30 p.m.	Fired 9 rds S.15.D.1.8. strafe	
	14/15 6 p.m.–7.30 p.m.		Fired 30 rds {S.15.D.1.8. / S.15.C.4.5.} Retaliation	
		6 p.m.–7 a.m.	Fired 25 rds ditto strafe	
		11.30/12	Fired 30 rds {S.15.D.1.8. / S.15.C.4.5.} Retaliation	
		7.30 a.m.	Fired 10 rds S.15.D.1.8. strafe	
		2.30 p.m.	Fired 3 rds S.15.C.6.3. Retaliation	
	16th	4 p.m.–5 p.m.	Fired 40 rds S.15.C.4.5. strafe	
	17th	7 a.m.	Fired 10 rds S.15.C.4.5. strafe	
		10.30 a.m.	Fired 10 rds S.15.C.4.5 + S.15.D.1.8. Retaliation	
		3 p.m.	Fired 23 rds S.15.C.6.3. strafe	
	18th	9 a.m.	Fired 9 rds S.15.C.4.5. to C.6.2.	
		12 a.m.	Fired 12 rds S.15.C.4.5. to C.6.2.	
	19th	8.30 a.m.	Fired 16 rds at points S.15.C.4.5 + S.15.D.1.8.	
		12.30 p.m.		
		2.15 p.m.	Fired 6 rds at points S.15.C.6.3.	

Army Form C. 2118.

X/24 TMB

WAR DIARY
or
INTELLIGENCE SUMMARY

(Erase heading not required.)

Instructions regarding War Diaries and Intelligence Summaries are contained in F. S. Regs., Part II. and the Staff Manual respectively. Title Pages will be prepared in manuscript.

Place	Date	Hour	Summary of Events and Information	Remarks and references to Appendices
	20th	8:45 a.m.	Fired 15 rds. at points S.15.C.4.5. (strafe)	
		11:30 a.m.	Fired 15 rds. at points S.15.C.3.5. Retaliation	
		3:15 p.m.	Fired 15 rds. at point Lady Groups (strafe)	
	21st	10-12:30	Fired 20 rds. at points S.15.C.4.5.	
		2:30 p.m.	Fired 22 rds. at point Lady Groups.	
	22nd	3:30 p.m.	Fired 3 rds.	
	23rd	10:15 a.m.	Fired 6 rds. at points S.15.C.4.5.	
	24th	5:45 a.m.	Fired 30 rds. at front line S.15.C.2.5 - 6.2.	
	25th	10 a.m. to 3:30 p.m.	Fired 80 rds. at Lady Groups and S.15.C.3.5. S.15.C.88. to S.15.D.0.8.	
	26th	4-18 a.m. to 12:30 p.m.	Fired 40 rds. at points S.15.C.88. to S.15.D.0.8.	
	27th	11:30 a.m.	Fired 39 rds. at Lady Groups.	
	28th	12:30 p.m.	Fired 33 rds. at S.15.C.3.5. and S.15.D.0.8.	
	29th	10:30 a.m.	Fired 20 rds. on front line S.15.C.35 to S.15.C.5.4 - Strafing - Many breaks were made in run parapet and some rounds dropped in enemy wire.	
		2:30 p.m.	Fired 30 rds. on Craters S.15.D.O.9 & S.15.D.18. - Strafing - Rounds most satisfactory upon the whole - some duds.	
	30th	10:15 a.m.	Fired 34 rds. on enemy front line S.15. C.3.5. to S.15. C.5.4. as strafe - several hits were obtained lifting duckboards and sandbags - Machine gunner have been acquainted.	

Army Form C. 2118.

X/24 T M B

WAR DIARY
or
INTELLIGENCE SUMMARY
(Erase heading not required.)

Instructions regarding War Diaries and Intelligence Summaries are contained in F. S. Regs., Part II. and the Staff Manual respectively. Title Pages will be prepared in manuscript.

Place	Date	Hour	Summary of Events and Information	Remarks and references to Appendices
	30th	2:30 p.m.	Fired 30 rds upon Crabio strafing. Rounds were all satisfactory apart from the fact that wind made observations impossible. Trenches had been repaired where they had partly subsided.	
	31st	2:30 to 4:30 p.m.	Fired 41 rds on front line S.15.C.3.5 to S.15.C.5.4. Fired 20 rds on supports (in triangle formed S.15.C.4.5. Fired 10 rds on Crabio (? Lady Trench) No wind came. 71 All rounds very satisfactory - Enemy front line again knocked about quite a lot and trench machine gunner observed damage with aid and is training guns on spot.	

S.J. Higgins Lt
O.C. X/24 T.M.B.

Army Form C. 2118.

Y/24 T.M.B.

WAR DIARY
or
INTELLIGENCE SUMMARY
(Erase heading not required.)

For OCT 1916

Instructions regarding War Diaries and Intelligence Summaries are contained in F. S. Regs., Part II. and the Staff Manual respectively. Title Pages will be prepared in manuscript.

Place	Date	Hour	Summary of Events and Information	Remarks and references to Appendices
Bruay	1.9.16	6 p.m.	Arrived Bruay	
	2.9.16	7 p.m.	Left Bruay for Camblain l'Abbé	
Camblain l'Abbé	Sept 3	5 p.m.	Reconnoitred new position on Vimy Ridge	
Vimy Ridge	4	1 p.m.	Relieved Y/9 T.M.B.	
	5	3.30 p.m.	Fired 6 rounds Registration	
	6	11 a.m.	Registered	
	7	1.30 p.m.	Fired 64 rounds stage registration	
	8	6.30 a.m.	Fired 20 rounds and commenced re-setting beds	
	9	9.15 a.m.	Fired 40 rounds Re-setting bed	
	10	3.30 p.m.	Fired 56 rounds Re-setting bed	
	11	12 noon	Fired 45 rounds Improved head cover and bomb store	
	12	2.15 p.m.	Fired 98 rounds Drained bomb store and began platform for bomb	
	13	1.0 p.m.	Fired 42 rounds Completed platform	
	14	9 a.m.	Fired 82 rounds	
	15	11.30 p.m.	Fired 30 rounds and repaired communication trench	
	16	2.45 p.m.	Fired 22 rounds Further communication trench	
	17	5.30 a.m.	Fired 47 rounds Reset beds	
	18	8.30 a.m.	Fired 31 rounds and enlarged bomb store	

WAR DIARY or INTELLIGENCE SUMMARY

Army Form C. 2118.

Instructions regarding War Diaries and Intelligence Summaries are contained in F.S. Regs., Part II and the Staff Manual respectively. Title Pages will be prepared in manuscript.

(Erase heading not required.)

Place	Date	Hour	Summary of Events and Information	Remarks and references to Appendices
Vimy	Sept 19	2p	Fired 33 rounds and laid telephone wires	
	20	8.15a	Fired 57 rounds. Repaired telephone line and lengthened same	
	21	4.3p	Fired 57 rounds and improved Observation Post in front line	
	22	9a	Fired 56 rounds. Took one dug up and rebuilt	
	23	7.35p	Fired 44 rounds and repaired trench which had caved in	
	24	6.30a	Fired 71 rounds and repaired communication trench between two 18 pr. gun pits	
	25	11.15a	Fired 53 rounds. Fired 9 belts away to short bursts	
	26	7.30p	Fired 36 rounds at enemy bomb	
	27	10a	Fired 48 rounds and repaired telephone line where broken. Altered arc of gun fit	
	28	11.15a	Fired 24 rounds and altered elevation of two beds getting wider arc of fire	
	29	3.30p	Fired 44 rounds and commenced repairing communication trenches which fell in	
	30	2.45p	Fired 30 rounds. Repaired & revetted communication trench	
	31	3.30p	Fired 54 rounds and repaired gun pit which had fallen in with heavy firing and bad weather	

J. Wentworth
2nd Lt R.F.A.
O.C. 7 M.G. M.G.B.

WAR DIARY or **INTELLIGENCE SUMMARY** For OcT 1916 Army Form C. 2118.

(Erase heading not required.)

Z/24 T.M.B.

Place	Date	Hour	Summary of Events and Information	Remarks and references to Appendices
Bruay	1	6 p.m.	Arrived at Bruay by train	
Cambelain l'Abbé	2	7 a.m.	Left Bruay by 'bus for Camblain-l'Abbé	
	3	5 p.m.	Went to Vimy Ridge to look round & ascertain best routes to get there.	
Vimy Ridge	4	9 a.m.	Trecked to Vimy Ridge & took over from 29 T.M.B. arriving at 5 p.m.	
"	5	do.	Registered no. 1 gun & inspected dugouts etc	
"	6	do.	tent wire at S.15.a.2 & 8 — 40 rds	
"	7	do.	tent wire at {S.15.a.2 & 9} {S.9.c.1,2 & 16} — 40 rds fired during rest by Seine on our point at {S.9.c.5,6,7 — 15 rds}	
"	8	7 p.m.	tent wire at S.9.c.1.2 — 1.6 — 100 rds with good effect making several large gaps damaging trench & gaps	
"	9	do.	Repeat no. 4 gun pit	
"	10	do.	fired on gun etc C.T's at S.9.c.24 gun wire at S.9.a.0.3–1/2.4 — 3 rds	
"	11	8 p.m.	Surprise fire at C.T junction at S.9.c.4.4 — 10 rds & at wire at S.9.a.4 — 2.55 — 20 rds initiated from S.9.a.3,7 & T junction	
"	12	7 p.m.	Registered 2 & 3 guns on wire from S.9.c.1,2 S.9.c.1.7. but wire at the trench S.9 at 4,20 rds each old do 4 gun on trench & wire from S.9.c.8–4.5 & S.9.c.13–7. The enemy fired about 10 pineapples	
"	13	7 p.m.	7 rounds fired today in retaliation of enemies fired on our artillery Bruden. 7 rounds fired from no. 5 installment, entering wire from S.9.a.1.5 S.9.c.1-6	
	14	6.30 a.m.	At 11 am. fired 96 during our artillery bombardment which lasted 40 min. on enemy front line between S.9.c.14 S.9.c.13.7. The usual retaliation to our installation 5 minues. fired at midday {Cut a gun in position left of Telefer batty. first aim 1507–2007 next}	

WAR DIARY
or
INTELLIGENCE SUMMARY

(Erase heading not required.)

Army Form C. 2118.

2/24 7. M. B.

Place	Date	Hour	Summary of Events and Information	Remarks and references to Appendices
Vimy Ridge	15		Heard the day on top of Vimy Ridge regarding a gun placed on the Pt. of Villers Arcourt, so 5 Bn were 10 rounds of 9. up 5 100 x south of the road at S.9 a 13. 2.9. Same evening the line motored above at S.9 a 5 - 7 - firing up into the 17 D.F.D. for enough point in the barrage on ammunition from Livin and Divy. Fired 79 Rds. G. day. S.O.S. from new village e 92 - 9; 19 Bt. half a minute shoot on the night of 15/16th from a 14 in retaliation to Germans.	
"	16		Quiet day @ No. 5. Had casual shot along new line S.9 c.2. — 17.3 Built new OP at a common jumbo above S.9 e . 5 and also dug repair gun pits & common jumbo.	
"	17		Fired 34 rds on new S.9 c.14.2 to 1.7 Shoot. My guns now on our central charge.	
"	18		Fired on snipers post at S.9 c.16.2. Ammunition wag. by 1 OR 2 D.night.	
"	19		Bullies were received at S8d 19.3.6.2 for a raid by 12 R.2. D. night.	
"	20		Fired 10 rds. at Aufen Coy. S.9 c.1.3.4. The 10th Can. a shoot at 4.40 a.m.	
"	21		to defensive amn. fell against him above by O. Pat. below.	
"	22		Fired 30 rds. at main along road at S8 d 19.3.6; No shorts to day as we have	
"	23		tried J-Tubes. I believe this trouble was due to faulty S.O.I. Bartridge.	
"	24		To-day weather very wet. Demolition is attempts on our new village. No firing.	
"	25		The opinion is that the demolition of the village is not worthwhile, as we shall relay all back for the time from so small efficacy of the Tok 2 min at only 2000 yds to & days. so further helped to each the gun over & mark the line exact.	

Army Form C. 2118.

WAR DIARY
or
INTELLIGENCE SUMMARY
(Erase heading not required.)

Z/24 T.M.B.

Place	Date	Hour	Summary of Events and Information	Remarks and references to Appendices
Vimy Ridge	26		The Canadian Infantry raid on "G" Division. The 4th Battalion of the Z/24 fired 26 rounds from No.5 – more satisfactory – damaged trench & made gap in wire around S9a1.8	
do.	27th		The wind much to gusty – a strong (S.W.) before 8 o'clock, headless on any day.	
do.	28th		Putting in new bed foundation. Fired 12rds this morning in retaliation to 5 Minnies. The afternoon having finished a cleaned emplacement & foundation on 3a, we fired 20rds. with excellent results.	
do	29th		Fired 8 rds in retaliation to 2 Minnies and made new emplacement for No 1.	
do	30th		Fired 6 rds registering No 1. (S15a2½.9) But registration not completed as wind was too strong for accurate fire	
do	31st		21 Rds. fired in registration in the not in barrage front line at S9a2.2	

J Thanks 2Lt
for OC Z24 TMB.

Army Form C. 2118.

N/24 T.M.B.

Vol 5

WAR DIARY
or
INTELLIGENCE SUMMARY.
(Erase heading not required.)

Instructions regarding War Diaries and Intelligence Summaries are contained in F. S. Regs., Part II. and the Staff Manual respectively. Title pages will be prepared in manuscript.

Place	Date	Hour	Summary of Events and Information	Remarks and references to Appendices
Army	1/11/16		Fired 63 rds on Enemy front line & supports.	
	2/11/16		Fired 103 rounds on Enemy front line & supports	
"	3/11/16		Fired 70 rounds on Crater and Saps. All my communication trenches in bad condition necessitating much work.	
"	4/11/16		Fired 45 rounds on Enemy front line and supports. All 8 bapt	
"	5/11/16		Fired 82 rounds on Crater & supports.	
"	6/11/16		Fired 63 rounds on Enemy front line & supports, also retaliation	
"	7/11/16		Fired 41 rounds on Snipers post completely destroyed same also front line & supports	
"	8/11/16		Fired 60 rounds on M.G. Emplacement & Listening Post. Good results. Emplacement completely destroyed	
"	9/11/16		Fired 51 rounds on M.G. Emplacement, destroyed same by 2 direct hits, also Enemy front line & supports.	
"	10/11/16		Fired 47 rounds on Enemy front line & supports. good results.	
"	11/11/16		Fired 68 rounds on front line & crater	
"	12/11/16		Fired 51 rounds on front line & ruby trench & crater. good results	

Army Form C. 2118.

WAR DIARY
or
INTELLIGENCE SUMMARY.
(Erase heading not required.)

Instructions regarding War Diaries and Intelligence
Summaries are contained in F.S. Regs., Part II.
and the Staff Manual respectively. Title pages
will be prepared in manuscript.

Place	Date	Hour	Summary of Events and Information	Remarks and references to Appendices
Vimy	13/1/16		Fired 68 rounds on Enemy front line & supports 10 in retaliation for minnies good results	
	14/1/16		Fired 4 rounds. Shortage of ammunition	
	15/1/16		Fired 68 rounds on Enemy front line & supports - co-operating with Y. Z. V and Stokes excellent results	
	16/1/16		Fired 26 rounds on Enemy front line & wire - good results - were also working on communication trenches in need of repair	
	17/1/16		Fired 60 rounds on Enemy front line & supports, also relaid telephone wire, as current was running to earth in several places	
	18/1/16		Fired 12 rounds on Enemy front line. Last round caused accident, details of which have already been forwarded by R.T. Smith	
	19/1/16		Fired 45 rounds on Enemy front line & supports good results	
	20/1/16		Fired 50 rounds on front line & craters have only 2 guns in action	
	21/1/16		Fired 50 rounds on front line & supports - good results	
	22/1/16		Fired 25 rounds on front line & supports - were repairing trenches	

Army Form C. 2118.

WAR DIARY
or
INTELLIGENCE SUMMARY.
(Erase heading not required.)

Place	Date	Hour	Summary of Events and Information	Remarks and references to Appendices
Vimy	23/11/16		Fired 60 rounds on front line and supports - good results	
"	24/11/16		Fired 60 rounds on front line and supports - Enemy retaliation which however done no damage.	
	25/11/16		Fired 51 rounds on front line and supports - very effective	
	26/11/16		Fired 30 rounds on front line & wire - good results	
	27/11/16		Fired 75 rounds on craters & front line & supports.	
	28/11/16		Fired 38 rounds on front line & supports - unobservable	
	29/11/16		Fired 26 rounds 16 in retaliation & remainder on Enemy front line.	
	30/11/16		Fired 42 rounds Enemy front line & support in retaliation and stops.	

WAR DIARY or INTELLIGENCE SUMMARY

Army Form C. 2118.

Y/24 TMB

Place	Date	Hour	Summary of Events and Information	Remarks and references to Appendices
Vimy	1.11.16		Fired 103 rounds on enemy front line supports. All my ammunition therein in but another necessitating much work.	
	2.11.16		Fired 50 rounds on enemy front line supports. Working on ammunition trench which has fallen in.	
	3.11.16		Fired 14 rounds with Livens. Fired further 88 rounds – Working in pits.	
	4.11.16		Fired 32 rounds only as the emplacements etc in an unsuitable condition owing to the rain.	
	5		Fired 66 rounds and reback telephone wires as current was earthing.	
	6		Fired 60 rounds and located 2 new observation posts for my use.	
	7		Fired 60 rounds doing much damage & throwing up trench rev...	
	8		Fired 68 rounds getting several direct hits.	
	9		Fired 46 rounds fired of them being in retaliation.	
	10		Fired 58 rounds drawing some retaliation which we silenced.	
	11		Fired 52 rounds. 32 being in retaliation. 20 of enemy output fire effective.	
	12		Fired 66 rounds strafe retaliation damaging enemy trenches.	
	14		Fired 12 rounds only, the men being employed in repairing damage to our communication trenches caused by recent heavy rain.	

Army Form C. 2118.

WAR DIARY
or
INTELLIGENCE SUMMARY.
(Erase heading not required.)

Instructions regarding War Diaries and Intelligence Summaries are contained in F. S. Regs., Part II. and the Staff Manual respectively. Title pages will be prepared in manuscript.

Place	Date	Hour	Summary of Events and Information	Remarks and references to Appendices
Henu	Mar 10		Fired 57 rounds in conjunction with Heavies Stokes	
	11		Fired 20 rounds on enemy wire	
	17		Fired 41 rounds on enemy wire. Front line system obtaining many direct hits	
	18		Fired 60 rounds on front line - effective shooting	
	19		Fired 50 rounds getting very effective bursts. The last week has been very much occupied in repairing trenches, head stores & emplacements. These are still in very bad state however & much more work is necessary	
	21		Fired 47 rounds. Erected out 4 trans wire to new O.P.	
	22		Fired 41 rounds & made new bed for dump. Two emplacements & Y dumholes	
	23		Fired 20 rounds - being with Stores	
	24		Fired 157 rounds 102 being as instructed	
	25		Fired 49 rounds on enemy wire. Being very effective burst	
	26		Fired 25 rounds. Enemy aeroplanes active & rly taken place. Envy very active on our left. One emplacement & Y trans in by enemy	
	27		Fired 87 rounds on enemy wire in preparation for raid	
	28		Fired 37 rounds according to programme. Buffoods stone blown up & telephone wires blown in & hand cut. Bften were damaged	
	29		Fired 20 rounds tolled effect with ammunition & small European phone connection	
	30		Fired 87 rounds in enemy support in conjunction with Stokes	

WAR DIARY or INTELLIGENCE SUMMARY

Army Form C. 2118.

2/24 T.M.B.

Place	Date	Hour	Summary of Events and Information	Remarks and references to Appendices
Vimy Ridge	1/11/16		25 Rds. fired this morning in registering no.1. gun front line aimed at S9c22.	
"	2/11/16		34 Rds. fired this afternoon by no.3 on front line aimed at S9a1t-7. 20 Rds. in retaliation. 6 Rds. fired at 1-9 a.m. on front line at S9c1t-2. to 5 minnies. 39 Rds. fired at 3 p.m. aimed at S9c1t-2 to S9c2t-11¼ pm. 18 Rds. fired in registration.	
"	3/11/16		21 Rds. fired in retaliation to 7 minnies. no 3a on S9c1t-4.	
"			15 Rds. fired on enemy's front line at 2 pm. aimed at S9c23. 15m, at at S9c1t-2 at 2 pm.	
"	4/11/16		53 Rds. fired in front line aimed at S9a1-3-15/ m from S9c1t-5. S9a1t-7. Wind very gusty left. at 24c13·15/ m from S9c1-5. S9c1t-7. S9c1-5. S9c1-7 to S9c22. among the damage done, the roof was blown in a heap. Officer wounded & man killed.	
"	5/11/16		23 Rds. fired in support in retaliation to 8 minnies. Wind too strong for accurate shooting. Fired 18 Rds. in retaliation 5 minnies fired & repeated no.2 on 20 rds. the killed enemy & made a direct hit on R.B.D.	
"	6/11/16		18 Rds. fired in retaliation to minnies. To day firing retaliation fire at 10·10 a.m. a premature occurred in 3a. killing 2 m-2 gtts, hit of gun. Probably due 27 Rds. fired in retaliation to 6 minnies. Weather miserable. to a bad charge. after 24 Rds. raining all day long. Fired 5 regts no.2 & had 6 stgs fired rain after 4 P.R.I. Fired 15 Rds. 6·1-2-4 pm. on front line at S9a1:? S9a1:?	
"	8/11/16		No.3 gun registered at S9a1-2, no.3 on front line from S9c22 to S9c1·5. 27 Rds. fired aimed at S9c1·7, in retaliation for 8 P.T. M's at 12·15/m-4·40/m-	

WAR DIARY or INTELLIGENCE SUMMARY

Army Form C. 2118.

Place	Date	Hour	Summary of Events and Information	Remarks and references to Appendices
Vimy Ridge	9/11/16		Arrived about 8 o'clock a.m. Officer in charge of Section Relieved 2/Lieut. [?]	
	10/11/16 11/11/16		Very clear day but did not do much firing on account of work to be done installing my post today but did some ranging on a machine gun emplacement at 59c2¾½ on which I fired 32 rds altogether. Fired 60 rds.	
do				
	12/11/16		Fired 16 rds. Today 8 rds in retaliation & 7 rds on M.G. Emplacement at 59c 3/11.½ Fired 19 rds in retaliation to Minnies and 23 rds on M.G. Emplacement at 59c 23/4.1/2 with splendid results. Hit 2 close of cover of emplacement. Shortly afterwards no (6) or emplacement hard to dump. Only 8 retaliation rds fired today.	
do	14/11/16		Today's work short, by Zwei. bombard 4.7" M. emplacement bombarders bombardment. First Heavy Artillery bombardment & Minnie emplacement hit 25 rds fired. Take place this afternoon at 1:30 p.m. as soon as we leave firing.	
do	15/11/16			
do	16/11/16		Heavy Artillery bombardment started. This afternoon at 2pm Firing 60 Rds. at bomb. Final. 25 35 22	
do	17/11/16		Too wet & windy - No observation.	
do	18/11/16		Fired in retaliation at 10:30 a.m. + Football	
do	19/11/16		Say to guns to No. 3 but have not enough ammn. due to Bangalorian Infantry carrying parties failing to turn up as asked.	

2449 Wt. W14957/M90 750,000 1/16 J.B.C. & A. Forms/C.2118/12.

WAR DIARY
or
INTELLIGENCE SUMMARY

(Erase heading not required.)

Army Form C. 2118.

2/24 T.M.B

Place	Date	Hour	Summary of Events and Information	Remarks and references to Appendices
Trine Hedge	20/11/16		Fired registering no 3 Winch gun from T.M.E.P. Stores as attached sample	
"	21/11/16		Fired 15-1 rds on enemy support & 10 day luntuction and defences	
"	22/11/16		Fired 18 rds in retaliation and 38 rds on supports	
"	23/11/16		Fired 6 rds in retaliation 43 rds at M.T.M. Emplacement at S9C3.5½	
"	24/11/16		Retaliated with 25 rds on M.T.M. Emplacement at S9C4.1½ and 24 rds stopping M.G. Emplacement at S9C3/4.1½	
"	25/11/16		Do a little Shoot on the front line with Stokes in the afternoon although raining all day no hits 30 rds.	
"	26/11/16		Only 27 Rds fired today on supports, as no catapult Shoots turned out on all this O.B.M's except one and that Touche as usual.	
"	27/11/16		50 Rds fired at S9c?.?. To night during a raid in which we blew up a mine.	
"	28/11/16		No Rds fired today. Enemy retaliated for last nights raid."	
"	29/11/16		Fired on Communication Trench S9C3.7½ i support at S9C3.4½ & S9C6½.6. Enemy retaliated at 11.30 A.M. & hit new cookhouse.	
"	30/11/16		Fired 30 rds on enemy Communication Trenches & supports from S9C.1.2 16 S9C3.7.	

Sam Browne Belt's

Nominal Roll /2.

24

X/24 TMB
Vol 6

WAR DIARY
or
~~INTELLIGENCE SUMMARY~~
(Erase heading not required.)

Army Form C. 2118.

Place	Date	Hour	Summary of Events and Information	Remarks and references to Appendices
Nemy	1st		Fired 48 rds. excellent burst	
	2nd		Fired 7 rds on Enemy Front line & supports	
	3rd		Fired 51 rds with good results	
Loos	4th		Half Battery relieved half battery of 40th Division	
	5th		Completed relief. Took over whole front covered by X/140	
	6th		Fired 38 rds retaliation	
	7th	" 45 "	very full retaliation	
	8th	" 24 "	Enemy arms gun positions	
	9th	" 40 "	Continued work on gun positions	
	10th	" 34 "	Offensive	
	11th	" 57 "	Retaliation	
	12th	" 42 "	On enemy front line & supports	
	13th	" 68 "	Offensive	
	14th	" 38 "	Support trencho	
	15th	" 51 "	Support good results obtained	
	16th	" 63 "	M.S.D. & M.G.E.	

Army Form C. 2118.

X/24 T MB

WAR DIARY
or
INTELLIGENCE SUMMARY.
(Erase heading not required.)

Instructions regarding War Diaries and Intelligence Summaries are contained in F. S. Regs., Part II. and the Staff Manual respectively. Title pages will be prepared in manuscript.

Place	Date	Hour	Summary of Events and Information	Remarks and references to Appendices
Loos	17"		Fired 76 rds - Offensive	
	18"		" 66 " Front line	
	19"		" 72 " Support line	
	20"		" 04 " Front line & Supports	
	21"		" 76 " Wire cutting	
	22"		" 41 " Several direct hits	
	23"		" 49 " Offensive	
	24"		" 45 " Front line	
	25"		" 66 " Christmas programme	
	26"		" 53 " Offensive	
	27"		" 62 " Supports - Offensive	
	28"		" 56 " Rifle mechanisms giving trouble	
	29"		" 22 " R.B. No still giving trouble	
	30"		" 12 " - ditto -	
	31"		All guns out of action owing to R.B. No all being broken	1 Q. D. atta Capt RM to O.C. X/24 TMB

3353 Wt.W.25441/7434 700,000 5/15 D. D. & L. A.D.S.S./Forms/C. 2118.

Army Form C. 2118.

Y/24 T M B

WAR DIARY
or
INTELLIGENCE SUMMARY
(Erase heading not required.)

Instructions regarding War Diaries and Intelligence Summaries are contained in F. S. Regs., Part II. and the Staff Manual respectively. Title pages will be prepared in manuscript.

Place	Date	Hour	Summary of Events and Information	Remarks and references to Appendices
Vermelles	1-12-16		Fired 52 rounds	
	2nd		" 106 " Relieved by 1/2 Battery of future Divn	
	3rd		Half battery out of action at Cambrin P'Able & the other half shooting for future Divn	
	4th		moved out half battery into action at Rullock - brought the 1/2 to Cambrin 1'Able	
	5th		fired 30 rounds and brought the remaining guns into action at Rullock	
	6th		" 35 rounds	
	7th		" 45 " Platform beginning to give	
	8th		" 35 " One platform taken up & reparation made for relaying same	
	9th		" 50 " Laying platform & starting up back of emplacement	
	10th		Fired 51 rounds on Enemy trenches & Sappers. Another platform requires relaying	
	11th		" 66 " 1st Platform relaid and work commenced on 2nd Back of	
	12th		" 58 " emplacement cannot stand strain & requires much work	
	13th		" 61 " Relaying platform and starting back of emplacement	
	14th		" 59 rounds and required entrance of emplacement which had been knocked in	
	15th		" 68 rounds and completed 2nd platform temporarily. One round dropped in groups but one 2 did	
	16th		" 65 " Shoul trouble with stock and have dropped one in our own	
			first line and went wounding 2 infantrymen	

2153 Wt. W:5344/1454 700,000 5/15 D. D. & L. A.D.S.S./Forms/C. 2118.

Army Form C. 2118.

Y/24 TMB

WAR DIARY
or
INTELLIGENCE SUMMARY.
(Erase heading not required.)

Instructions regarding War Diaries and Intelligence Summaries are contained in F.S. Regs., Part II. and the Staff Manual respectively. Title pages will be prepared in manuscript.

Place	Date	Hour	Summary of Events and Information	Remarks and references to Appendices
	14th Feb 16		Front H5 round (cont) Front of our emplacement which is facing in wrong direction (negociating) + work is being done as fast as possible upon this	
	16th	56 "	Altering direction of emplacement	
	18th	45 "		
	19th	38 "		
	20th	62 "	" Casualty - Gunner Wills (Killed) + Gnr. Kelly wounded.	
	21st	51 "	Front of emplacement now found in correct direction; and as Enemy Bombardment Hullock Sector.	
	22nd	40 "	is now being altered/turned.	
	23rd	70 "	to traverse, bed having to extend 9'6". is now put in the altered emplacement	
	24th	68 "		
		9½ "	abandoned in trench bombardment with artillery	
	25th	60 "	"	
	26th	61 "	Our gun emplacement destroyed by minenwerfer and	
	27th	30 "	trench made impassable by day. Digging out the gun at night	
	28th	46 "	Digging out gun. Target telephone wires to O.P.	
	29th	41 "	Dropped 1 round on fort line + burst a gap behind. Caused by gun firing	
	30th	43 "	Digging out gun under possible but minenwerfer + 4.2 keep on the spot at intervals day + night	
	31st			

Alvesta Browne
O.C. 4 Hy TMB
2nd Feb 1916

2351 Wt W2541/1454 700,000 5/15 D.D.&L. A.D.S.S./Forms/C. 2118.

Army Form C. 2118.

Z/24 TMB

WAR DIARY
or
INTELLIGENCE SUMMARY.
(Erase heading not required.)

Instructions regarding War Diaries and Intelligence Summaries are contained in F. S. Regs., Part II. and the Staff Manual respectively. Title pages will be prepared in manuscript.

Place	Date	Hour	Summary of Events and Information	Remarks and references to Appendices
Vimy	Dec 1	9 pm	Fired 34 rounds	
"	" 2	7.30	Fired 41 rounds, Relieved by half Batty of Lahore Divn	
"	" 3		Half Battery at actn of Canadian mning Coy assisting Lahore Div	
Lens	" 4	7.30 am	Relieved left sector of 2/40 TMB at 14 Bde.	
"	" 5	7 pm	Relieved night sector of 2/40 TMB at 14 Bde fired 19 rds with good effect	
"	" 6	9 am	Relayed gun at Seaford Alley, and repaired own tunnel	
"	" 7	9.30	finished relaying SP gun at Seaford Alley stated new position in Canary	
"	" 8	2.15 pm	Fired 34 rounds (two direct hits)	
"	" 9	9.30 am	Fired 53 rds, mine cutting	
"	" 10	11-0 am	Fired 49 rds, also repaired implements	
"	" 11	12 noon	Fired 52 rounds, Rifle Barrel Mechanism giving a lot of trouble	
"	" 12	8.30 pm	Fired 64 rounds, several direct hits / timber were thrown well in air	
"	" 13	10.20 am	Fired 95 rounds, 20 of these were front wire absence (night firing)	
"	" 14	3.30 pm	Fired 96 rounds	
"	" 15	11.15 am	Fired 66 rounds TRBM again gave trouble	
"	" 16	1.30	Fired 64 rounds, Gun Pit damaged by minenwerfer	

WAR DIARY
~~INTELLIGENCE SUMMARY~~

(Erase heading not required.)

Army Form C. 2118.

Z/24 TMB

Place	Date	Hour	Summary of Events and Information	Remarks and references to Appendices
Sars	Dec 17	3h	Fired 16 rounds on front line	
	" 18	4pm	Fired 64 rounds (good result)	
	" 19	3.30	Fired 96 rounds (Artillery Offensive)	
	" 20	9.15am	Fired 23 rounds Offensive (ruptured gun positions)	
	" 21	8.15	Fired 30 rounds enemy front line N.19.27	
	" 22	4pm	Fired 40 rounds Enemy Sap/ents	
	" 23	4.15pm	Fired 43 rounds (Boche Stove team Position destroyed) gas shelley	
	" 24	8.30am	Fired 10 rounds Sars Buried by shell fire)	
	" 25	11am	Fired 57 rounds (started to reinstate gun position)	
	" 26	12.15p	Fired 25 rounds (Fired and silenced several shell Pits	
	" 27	2pm	Working on new position	
	" 28		Not engaged owing to RBMs out of action) still working on new position	
	" 29	11.30am	Fired 36 rounds Offensive	
	" 30		Unable to fire all RBMs out of action	
	" 31	8.30am	Started new on repairing gun position in Quarry	

H.Polvinicy Lieut
OC Z/24 TMB

18th Army Field Artillery Brigade.	New Nomenclature of Battys.
59th, 94th & D/16 (How) Btty; from Res. Arty. 1 Sect. (4.5" How), from Fifth Army.	59th, 94th, A/18 (18 pdr) D/18 (How).

The present Headquarters of the 18th Field Artillery Brigade will form the Headquarters of the 18th Army Field Artillery Brigade.

D. **AMMUNITION COLUMNS.**

The Divisional Ammunition Columns will be reconstituted as shown in para. 9 of O.B/1866, the third section of "A" Echelon of each Divisional Ammunition Column being withdrawn to form the Ammunition Columns of the Army Field Artillery Brigades, and to bring the existing Divisional Ammunition Columns up to the new establishment, as follows :-

I CORPS.

No.3 Sect. 6th D.A.C. will form the Amm.Col for the 38th A.F.A.Bde.

No.3 Sect. 24th   "   "   "   "   "   "   " 108th   "   "

No.3 Sect. 21st   "   will be broken up, and this personnel, together with that to be withdrawn from "B" Echelon will be used to complete the establishment of the 38th and 108th Army Field Artillery Brigade Ammunition Columns, and bring the present D.A.C's. in the I Corps up to the new establishment.

XI CORPS.

No.3 Sect. 5th D.A.C. will form the Amm.Col. for the 28th A.F.A.Bde.

No.3 Sect. 56th   "   "   "   "   "   "   " 282nd   "   "

No.3 Sect. 37th   "   " be broken up, and the personnel, together with that to be withdrawn from "B" Echelon will be used to complete the establishment of the 28th and 282nd Army Field Artillery Brigade Ammunition Columns, and bring the present D.A.C's. of the XI CORPS up to the new establishment.

CANADIAN CORPS.

No.3 Sect. Reserve D.A.C. will form the Ammunition Column for the 18th Army Field Artillery Brigade; This Ammunition Column, and also the existing Reserve D.A.C. will be brought up to their new establishment by the personnel to be withdrawn from "B" Echelon and by surplus from I and XI Corps, the remainder being demanded from the Base.

(ii)   After carrying out these redistributions, Corps will report all deficiencies and surplus under the different headings as shewn in War Establishments, as follows :-

```
Personnel - except A.S.C. personnel - to FIRST ARMY "A".
Transport -                         - D.D.S.&.T.  FIRST ARMY.
Vehicles & complete turn out &
         A.S.C. personnel           - to DYD.S.&.T. FIRST ARMY.
Horses, other than above -          - to D.D.R.    FIRST ARMY.
```

(4).

(iii)   Appendix "A" shows the total personnel that should be surplus or deficient according to establishment in each Corps (I & XI) after re-organisation.

Appendix "B" shows the surplus per I and XI Corps on forming two Army Brigade Ammunition Columns.

E.   On completion of re-organisation, Army Artillery Brigades will be attached for administration as follows :-

I Corps.

    38th Army Field Artillery Brigade.
    108th "   "   "   "

XI Corps.

    28th   "   "   "   "
    232nd "   "   "   "

CANADIAN CORPS.

    18th   "   "   "   "

F.   Surplus Brigade Headquarters will remain for the present under the orders of the Corps in which they are located.

G.   The new re-organisation will be carried out forthwith and the report called for in para 3D" (ii) will be forwarded as soon as possible, so that the Reserve Artillery may know what personnel will be available to meet their requirements.

The personnel, which it can be seen from Appendix "A" will not be available within the Army, should be demanded from the Base as soon as it can be conveniently allotted.

Headquarters,   Signed. F.H.DANSEY, Lieut-Colonel,
First Army.   A.A.G., First Army.

APPENDIX "A".

DIVISIONAL AMMUNITION COLUMN.

Nos. 1, 2, Sections each.	Present Establishment. "A" Echelon. PERSONNEL. Nos. 1 & 2 Secs. each.				New Establishment. "A" Echelon. PERSONNEL. Nos. 1 & 2 Secs. Combined.				Total deficiencies in "A" Echelon (2 Sections) on reconstruction, i.e. per Division.				Surplus from Appx. "B" set off against deficiencies.	Final Result. Surplus+ Deficiency+
	Officers	S/Sergts. or A.Q.Ms.	Artificers etc.	Rank & file	Total	Officers	S/Sergts. or A.Q.Ms.	Artificers	Rank & file	Total	Officers	S/Sergts. or A.Q.Ms. Artificers etc.	Rank & file	Total	Personnel	Personnel
Captain	1				1	1				1					1	1
Subalterns	2				2	3				3	2				6	6+
R.S.M.		1			1		1			1					1	1
R.Q.M.S.		1			1		1			1					1	1
Sergts.		4			4		5			5		2			4	2+
Farrier Sgts.		1			1		1			1					1	1
Shoeing Smiths.			6		6			6		6			2		6	4+
Saddlers.			2		2			3		3			2		6	7+
Fitters or Whlr.			1		1			2		2			2		6	1+
Corporals.				4	4				6	6				2	6	4+
Bombdrs.				5	5				6	6				3	6	3+
Gunners.				45	45				50	50				10	30	92 62
Drs. (For vehicles.)				101	101				114	114				26	78	154 76
Drs. (For spare drt.)				8	8				11	11				6	18	14+ 4
Drs. (For spare)				4	4				5	5				2	6	4+
Batmen.				3	3				4	4				2	6	5+ 1
Dvrs. A.S.C.(Train Transport).				2	2				5	5				6	18	20+ 2+
TOTAL	3	1	5	9 172	● 190	4	1	6	12 200	● 223	2		2 6 56		● 66 198	273 20+

● Totals include A.S.C.

Deficiencies marked thus +

APPENDIX "B".

No. 3 Section of 3 Div. Ammun. Col. combined.	Present Establishment. "A" Echelon per Section. TOTALS per Division.					New Establishment A.F.A.Bde.Ammn.Col. TOTAL for 2 Ammn. Columns. 2 Army Arty. Bde. Ammn. Col.					Surplus per Corps on formation of 2A.F.A. Bdes. Ammn. Columns.					Add. surplus withdrawn from "B" Echelon D.A.Cs.(3 Dvns)	Total surplus to be set off against deficiencies in Appendix "A".
	PERSONNEL.					PERSONNEL.					PERSONNEL.					PERSONNEL.	PERSONNEL.
	Officers.	W. Os. Staff Sgts. & Sgts.	Artificers.	Rank & File.	TOTAL.	Officers.	W. Os. Staff Sgts. & Sgts.	Artificers.	Rank & File.	TOTAL.	Officers.	W. Os. Staff Sgts. & Sgts.	Artificers.	Rank & File.	TOTAL.		
Captain.	1				5	1				2	1				1		1
Subalterns.	2				6	3				6					–		–
B.S.M.		1			3		1			2		1			1		1
R.Q.M.S.		1			3		1			2		1			1		1
Sergts.		4			12		4			8		4			4		4
Farrier Sergts.			1		3			1		2			1		1		1
Shoeg. Smiths.			5		15			5		10			5		5		5
Saddlers.			2		6			2		4			2		2		2
Fitters & whlrs.			1		3			2		4			–1+		–1+		–1+
Corporals.				4	12				5	10				2	2		2
Bombardiers.				5	15				6	12				3	3		3
Gunners.				45	135				35	70				65	65	27	92
Drivers (for vehicles).				101	305				106	212				91	91	63	154
Drivers (for spare dgt.)				8	24				10	20				4	4		4
Drivers (for spare).				4	12				15	10				2	2		2
Batmen.				3	9				4	8				1	1		1
Drs.A.S.C.(Train Transport).				2	6				4	8				2	2		–2+
TOTAL.	3	5	9	175	570	4	5	10	175	390	1	1	5 8 –1+	168 –2+	183 –3+	90	273

Deficiencies marked thus +

O.B.1866.

FIRST ARMY.

Reference O.B./1866 dated 21st December 1916, para 11, last two lines,

for "1 - 18-pr. Battery from First Army to Second Army.
1 - 18-pr. Battery from Fifth Army to Third Army."

read "1 - 18-pr. Battery from First Army to Third Army. *
1 - 18-pr. Battery from Fifth Army to Second Army."

* This will be the 122nd Field Battery now detached with Third Army.

(Sd) J. BURNETT-STUART. B.G.
General Headquarters.   for Lt. General. C.G.S.
25/12/16.

WAR DIARY or INTELLIGENCE SUMMARY

Army Form C. 2118.

Place	Date	Hour	Summary of Events and Information	Remarks and references to Appendices
Hulluch	1917 Oct 1	Fired 37 rds.	Fired on Enemy Front line & Supports in H.13.c & H.19.A.	Offensive
	" 2	34 "	— do —	— do —
	" 3	25 "	Fired on Enemy Front line & more from H.13.c.55 to H.19.A.8.4.	Offensive & retaliation
	" 4	45 "	— do —	Offensive and preparation for future operations
	" 5	30 "	— do —	— do —
	" 6	15 "	Fired on Enemy Front line & Supports in H.19.D.	Retaliation
	" 7	28 "	— do — (H.13.c.) Registered HOLLY LANE (not found).	Offensive
	" 8	25 "	Fired on Enemy Wire at H.13.c.53.0	(preparation for future operations)
	" 9	29 "	— do — H.13.c.53.0	— do —
	" 10	121 "	Cut Wire near Sap HS (H.13.c.55.0) Fired in conjunction with raids (H.13. & H.19.A)	
	" 11	38 "	Fired on Enemy Support line from H.19.A.9.9 to H.19.B.0.2.	Offensive
	" 12	45 "	Front line & Support in H.13.c & H.19.A	— do & retaliation
	" 13	44 "	— do —	+ H.19.D
	" 14	40 "	— do —	Offensive
	" 15	– "	— do —	
	" 16	69 "	— do — in H.13.c.	— do —

Army Form C. 2118.

WAR DIARY
or
INTELLIGENCE SUMMARY.
(Erase heading not required.)

7/24 MB

Place	Date	Hour	Summary of Events and Information	Remarks and references to Appendices
	1917 Jan'y 17		Grid 43 ords. Fired on Enemy front line from H.13.c.5½.4 to H.19.a.5½.8	Offensive
	18		— do —	Offensive retaliation
	19	52	Fired on Enemy front line & support in H.13.C.	— do —
	20	49	— do — in H.19.A.	— do —
	21	39	Fired on Enemy front line & were from H.13.C.5½.4 to H.19.a.5½.9.	Offensive
	22	11	— do —	— do —
	23	73	Preparation for future operation. Cuts were at H.19.A.6.8 *	
	24		— do — — do — H.19.A.6.9 -	
	25	40	Repelled Vendin (new position) Various support Batteries in conjunction with raid near Sap #5.	
	26	36	Fired on Enemy front line & support in H.19.A.	Offensive retaliation
	27	20	— do —	Retaliation on guns on Crompton Bar D.A
	28	46	Fired on Enemy front line + support in H.19.D + H.19.A.	Offensive
	29	12	H.19.A	— do —
	30	10	— do —	— do —
	31		— do — H.13.C.	

10 Mounted 2/2 RFA
9/24 JM BS

WAR DIARY or INTELLIGENCE SUMMARY

Army Form C. 2118.

Z/24 T.M.B.

Place	Date	Hour	Summary of Events and Information	Remarks and references to Appendices
Map 51 c H.25 & 28	1/2/17	11. A.M.	Fired on Trench mortar emplacement 3.10 repeated operation	Retaliation
	2/2/17	3.15 pm	Wire cutting at H.25.c.9½.1.	
	3/2/17	11. A.M.	Retaliation on Trench mortar emplacement. H.25.d.8.8.	
		2.30 pm	" " N.25.d.8.8.	
	4/2/17	10.30am	Fired on enemy working party	
	5/2/17	5 A.M.	Enemy penetrated our line at H.25.c.8.7, we killed 8 men & officer	
		2. pm	Retaliation for wire cutting at H.25.c.9½.½	
	6/2/17	2 pm	" " at H.25.c.6.6.3.	
	9/2/17	10 A.M.	Wire cutting H.25.d.7.3. enemy quiet	
	10/2/17	2 pm	Wire Cutting. Enemy quiet.	
	11/2/17	10. A.M.	Wire Cutting H.25.c.9½.½ retaliation from enemy 3.H.T.M. on do	
	12/2/17	11.30	Retaliation on Trench mortar emplacement H.25.d.53.	
	13/2/17	2.1 pm	Wire cutting H.22.c.9½.½ Retaliation from enemy T.M.	
	14/2/17	10.30 pm	V.C. Reported the raid north 90 Posts everything caught	
	15/2/17	11 AM	Heavy T. M. shelling to day H.25. No casualty	
	16/2/17		Enemy shelling very quiet	

Army Form C. 2118.

2/24 TMB

WAR DIARY
or
INTELLIGENCE SUMMARY.

(Erase heading not required.)

Instructions regarding War Diaries and Intelligence Summaries are contained in F.S. Regs., Part II. and the Staff Manual respectively. Title pages will be prepared in manuscript.

Place	Date	Hour	Summary of Events and Information	Remarks and references to Appendices
	17/1/17	10 AM	Heavy Artillery shelling and fire enemy retaliation.	
	18/	3 AM	Our Artillery very active. Enemy very quiet. Both sides quiet.	
	19/1/17		H.T.M's in [Lohali] Rt. fired in retaliation to 14 Bie 1.30 [Sec]	
	20/1/17	9 AM		
	21/1/17	10.30 AM	Field artillery shelling tour about 40. 4/26 + 50. 77 MM.	
	22/1/17	11 AM	Retaliation for Kartile T.M. 40 rounds.	
	23/1/17	3 PM	Enemy artillery very quiet. We retaliated for T.M.	
	24	11 AM	Registration of all our guns on enemy trench.	
	25	10 AM	Good work on wire cutting. Enemy attitude quiet.	
	26	1.45 AM	We expected the raid with 180 rounds.	
	27/1/17	12 noon	Few T.M's on left. Generally very quiet.	
	28/1/17	2.6pm + 5.30pm	27 rds on Mini Shaft at N.1.a.3.5.5.2. 10 rds	
			T.M's very active 3.0 pm	
	29/1/17	11.0 am	20 rds on Fine Shaft & Front line. No retaliation.	
		2.20 pm	Explosion in H060 Lane Location.	
	30/1/17		No firing owing to relief. Fired 17 rds at noon.	
	31/1/17		Fired 50 rds for 14 Bie and general moral vector.	

[signed] Hflaw 2/LT RFA
OC 2/24 TMB

Army Form C. 2118.

24th Div "Amm" Column Sheet 1.
Vol 18

WAR DIARY
or
INTELLIGENCE SUMMARY.
(Erase heading not required.)

Instructions regarding War Diaries and Intelligence Summaries are contained in F. S. Regs., Part II. and the Staff Manual respectively. Title pages will be prepared in manuscript.

Place	Date	Hour	Summary of Events and Information	Remarks and references to Appendices
Head Qrs HOUCHIN Map 36/G	1917 July 1		Weather fine cloudy at first sunny later; first continues Intoxulence Clear wind NE light Posted D/118 at 2.1 & 6.15p from attached B Echelon and 13 gunners to Brigades RFA. Fig. 2.15 pm 2 Horn gro from B Echelon. 2. H.m. pm from Fr 1 Sec. The new gunners to 107, Bm RFA Amm 16/h gunners to 108, 13th gunners 9 2 Sec to 107, 108 RFA	G.T
	2		Weather fine Clear, train front wind light NE. supplied 2 E.S Waggons for transport of ammunition Lieut H. Pine Clarke vacated Adjutancy of DAC on posting to 117/13th RFA. 2/Lieut R.R. Penn assumed duties of Adjutant — anthems guns from 24 RA Sec. HQ 16/7 2.8.17.	G.T
	3		Weather fine bright early, sunny later hard frost. Wind NE light supplied 17 GS waggons both field & amm for transport of ammunition	G.T

T.134. Wt. W708–776. 500000. 4/16. Sir J. C. & S.

Army Form C. 2118.
Sheet 2.

WAR DIARY
or
INTELLIGENCE SUMMARY.
(Erase heading not required.)

Place	Date	Hour	Summary of Events and Information	Remarks and references to Appendices
	1917			
Head Qrs	Feb 4th		Weather fine, clear with dim sunshine. Wind NE Light. Calm. Parking G.S.W. Supplied 17 G.S. Wagons with full teams for Transport of Ammunition:- 2 2nd⁰/L Manifold field to A. Battery R.A. 2 2/Lieut	E.T.
HUCHIN			B.A. Ship and Padeth 2m Div. Train went on leave:-	
	5th		Weather fine. Some snow during day. 4-5° Clear with Sunshine at times. Wind NE Light Medium Supplied 26 Wagons G.S. with full teams for transport of ammunition:-	E.T.
	6th		Weather fine with Sun and some mist Transport Wind NE Light Supplies 32 G.S. Wagons with transport of Ammunition.	E.T.
	7th		Weather fine, clear, sunny. Hand frost. Wind NE Light & Camp:- Sent 2 Sngts 2 Corporals 2 2nd⁰/L & 40 Gunners & Drivers R.F.A. in exchange for similar numbers. Sent 3 O.R.S. to work with Inland Water transport to ROUEN also 1 O.R. to advanced horse depot for Road Construction Work. Supplied 25 G.S. Wagons for Ammunition transport.	E.T.
	8th		Weather fine, clear, sunny. hard frost. Wind NE Light & Calm Supplied 21 G.S. Wagons with full teams for transport of Ammunition:-	E.T.

Army Form C. 2118.

Sheet 3

WAR DIARY
or
INTELLIGENCE SUMMARY.

(Erase heading not required.)

Instructions regarding War Diaries and Intelligence Summaries are contained in F. S. Regs., Part II. and the Staff Manual respectively. Title pages will be prepared in manuscript.

Place	Date	Hour	Summary of Events and Information	Remarks and references to Appendices
HOULLE	1917 Jan 9		Weather fine cold clear sunny wind NE light & calm. Supplied 26 G.S. waggons with free trains for transport of ammunition.	G.T.
	10th		Weather fine cold clear and sunny hoar frost wind NE light & calm. Supplied 25 waggons with full teams for ammunition transport.	G.T.
	11th		Weather fine cold wind NE N.E. clear with sunshine some cloud. Supplied 47 waggons for transport of ammunition.	G.T.
	12		Weather fine overcast misten wind light N & NE supplied 1 G.S. waggon for transport of ammunition.	G.T.
	13th		Weather fine less cold wind NW light thaw & slight frost at night.	
		12 non	The 24th DAC marched on five roads to billets at BOURECQ. Personnel accommodated in farms in village, horses in fields in open.	Map 38 A. App. 43.

T.1134. Wt. W708-776. 500000. 4/15. Sir J. C. & S.

Army Form C. 2118.

Sheet 4

WAR DIARY
or
INTELLIGENCE SUMMARY.
(Erase heading not required.)

Instructions regarding War Diaries and Intelligence Summaries are contained in F. S. Regs., Part II and the Staff Manual respectively. Title pages will be prepared in manuscript.

Place	Date	Hour	Summary of Events and Information	Remarks and references to Appendices
Hd Qrs	14th			
BOURECQ	14th		Weather fine sunny. Wind N.t.N.E. Calm. Front at night: In our trench refitting out. Carried out programme of drills &c. 19 other ranks joined from Base.	G.T.
Map 36A				
"	15		Weather fine Cold. Sunny. Some haze early. Late frost at night. Wind N.t.N.E light & calm. 11 L.D. Penta and 3 indus joined.	G.T
"	16th		Weather fine Cold. Sunny from haze early and late frost at night wind N.t.N.E light to calm.	
"	17th		Weather fine dull. Thaw. Some snow and slight rain. A.D. wind W light. Puddle sent 2 Lewis machines and 13 O.R.s L.P. A.S.O. Trench S.P.Bn. 2nd School.	
"	18		Fine. Cloudy with rain in showers. Thaw. Conditions of mud. W light. Supplies 3 G.S. Wagons with fruit ??? to R.A. Hqrs. O.R.s Cmds. 6 Pr Trench Mortar & Mortars	G.T.

T.134. Wt. W708-776. 500000. 4/15. Sir J. C. & S.

WAR DIARY
INTELLIGENCE SUMMARY.

Army Form C. 2118.

Sheet 5.

Place	Date	Hour	Summary of Events and Information	Remarks and references to Appendices
	1917			
Head Qrs	Feb 19		Weather dull, mostly fintour, Showing wind WK NW. Sent 1 officer 87 ORs. 12 g. horses and mules and 30 G.S. S.A.A. wagons empty on special duty to HERSIN to report to Town Major there:- drew up 882 OTP 2do S.A.A in horse lts 73 echelon wagons twice at	MAP 36TB
MANQUE-VILLE. Map 36 A.			BOURECQ at T 6 d. q. 5. Map 36 A. Sent 1 officer and 50 ORs to T.R.T. at 1.17. Map 36 B to report to O/C 560 Coy R.E. A.T. The Column marched to the two Columns as under. Hd Qrs and B Echelon to MANQUEVILLE. U.2.7. Map 36A. No 1 Section to LE CORNET BRASSART. 0.23.C. No 2 Section to LE CORNET BOURDOIS 0.24.C. Map 36 A.:- 2/Lieut C.R.C. Lloyd joined and posted to No 1 Section:-	App. 44
"	Feb 20		Weather Rainy Wind W to NW brisk. Held heavy rain during night f. 20 - 2 f.f. : Incurred much:- 2/Lieut Harris posted to V Train Hunter Battery.	L.T.
"	Feb 21		Weather dull foggy warm. Wind S.W. Light:- posted 1.S.S. & 108 D.OK R.F.A and 12.C.R.S. Ope D.T. Perman 1107 Rect;	O.T.

WAR DIARY
or
INTELLIGENCE SUMMARY
(Erase heading not required.)

Army Form C. 2118.

Sheet 6

Place	Date	Hour	Summary of Events and Information	Remarks and references to Appendices
	1917			
Head Qrs MANQUEVILLE	Feb 23rd		Weather dull, rainy. Wind W. & S.W. Light. Capt. A.W. LYLE-KIDD assumed command of Column during temporary absence of Lt. Col. G. Talbot who left on leave to England at 12 noon.	R.
Head Qrs MANQUEVILLE	Feb 24th		Weather dull and mild. Wind S.W. Lt. 42 O.R. arrived as reinforcements from the Base. 2nd Lieut. G. Meagan joined from 42nd Bde R.F.A. 6 horses.	R.
"	Feb 25th		Weather fine in morning turning to dull in the afternoon. Wind W. N.W. Light. Reinforcements who arrived yesterday posted 2nd Lt. Meagan posted to No 2 section. O.R. as follows - 4 Gr. & 10 Dr. to No 1 Sec. 4 Gr. & 5 Dr. to No 2 Sec. and 4 Gr. and 11 Dr. to "B" Echelon. The remaining Lt. (Harvey) was sent to R.A. H.Qrs as Liaison of C.R.A. 2nd Lt G. Meagan posted to No 2 Sec.	R.
"	Feb 26th		Weather fine. Wind N.W. very Lt. Supplied 1 senior N.C.O. and 16 men to proceed to BOURECQ and thence in lorries to AOCHY-au-BOIS to Jalijine Farm to be attached to New at-tachee place by Brigade Major R.A. 24th Divn. Supplied 16 wagons to transport Horse BOURECQ and thence in lorries to KAOCHY-au-BOIS to Jalijine Farm to be attached to New at-tachee place by Brigade Major R.A. 24th Divn. Supplied 16 wagons to transport 2 drivers detailed to Transportation Depot BOULOGNE. Competition in Divnal of Cross-Country Race.	R.

Army Form C. 2118.

WAR DIARY
or
INTELLIGENCE SUMMARY.
(Erase heading not required.)

Instructions regarding War Diaries and Intelligence Summaries are contained in F. S. Regs., Part II. and the Staff Manual respectively. Title pages will be prepared in manuscript.

Place	Date	Hour	Summary of Events and Information	Remarks and references to Appendices
Head Qrs MANQUE- VILLE	Feb 27		Weather fine, dull cold wind N.N.W. very light. Supplied fatigue party of 31 mounted men to 106th Fd Ambce. ESCAUDECQUES for range clearing and road clearing. Patrols 6 O.R. + 12 Ummers to 106th Bde and 4 O.R. + 12 Ummers to 107th Bde.	Sheet 7. QR
"		Feb 28	Weather fine, dull. Wind N. light. Supplied fatigue party of 31 mounted to 106th Bgde for same purpose as yesterday. Lt. Maddison + 10 O.R. returned from tour Army French Motor School. 3 O.R. leaving gone into hospital there. Sent 7 O.R. to next course at Same School.	QR

In the Field

R Cooper Keene Capt.
for C.O. 24th D.A.C.
1st March 1917.

Y/24 1MB Army Form C. 2118.

Sheet 1

WAR DIARY
or
INTELLIGENCE SUMMARY.
(Erase heading not required.)

Instructions regarding War Diaries and Intelligence Summaries are contained in F.S. Regs., Part II. and the Staff Manual respectively. Title pages will be prepared in manuscript.

Place	Date	Hour	Summary of Events and Information	Remarks and references to Appendices
HINGES	1.2.17		Leads to/made	
	2"		24 "	French Junction at H.13.c.7.4.
	3"		26 "	Enemy Wire at H.19.A.60.45.
	4"		nil	" Front line H.19.A.7.7.
	5"		15 "	Communication trench H.13.c.6.8.
	6"		50 "	Front line & Wire. H.19.A.7.6.
	7"		30 "	Enemy Wire. H.19.A.65.60
	8"		50 "	Wire H.19.A.65.60
	9"		71 "	Wire H.19.c.9.8.
	10"		28 "	Front line H.19.D. — Gap made
	11"		10 "	— do —
	12"		nil	— " —
	13"		Handed over to 2/34 I.M.B.	
LESPESSE	14"	8.0a	Proceed to LESPESSE for Divisional Rest.	
	16&17		At LESPESSE	
	18		Moved to HAM EN ARTOIS	

Army Form C. 2118.

WAR DIARY
or
INTELLIGENCE SUMMARY.
(Erase heading not required.)

Sheet E

Place	Date	Hour	Summary of Events and Information	Remarks and references to Appendices
Hamel en Artois	18 to 20		Divisional Rest.	

McManus D. 2/C P.R.
O.C. 1/2 D. Ln 98

2/24" TMB
Sheet No 1

WAR DIARY
or
INTELLIGENCE SUMMARY.
(Erase heading not required.)

Army Form C. 2118.

Place	Date	Hour	Summary of Events and Information	Remarks and references to Appendices
doos	1/2/17		Fired 20 Rds in retaliation on 14 Bde with good effect	
do	2/2/17		Fired 30 Rds on enemy supports at H25c40.50 and 20 rds on front line at M1a40.50	
do	3/2/17		Retaliated on Support line at M1a 40.80 and fired 20 rds on 14 Bde.	
"	4/2/17		Battery out of action owing to heck of R.B.H's ammunition	
"	6/2/17	2 p.m.	12 rounds on new N.J. GORDON CRATER.	
"	7/2/17	11.30 p.m.	Wire cutting H.J. PUITS 14 BIS & N.J. GORDON CRATER	
"	8/2/17	2.30 p.m.	Fired 30 rds on wire N.J. PUITS 14 BIS.	
"	9/2/17	11.30 p.m.	15 rds on new PUITS 14 BIS. Battery out of action.	
"	10/2/17		Battery out of action. no R.B.M.	
"	11/2/17	11.30 p.m.	Raid cancelled. did not fire in consequence.	
"	12/2/17		Fired many offensive & night shoots about 100 rds. or come out	
"	13/2/17	4 p.m.	Division came out of action from Loos Right.	

Army Form C. 2118.

Sheet No. 2

WAR DIARY
or
INTELLIGENCE SUMMARY.
(Erase heading not required.)

Place	Date	Hour	Summary of Events and Information	Remarks and references to Appendices
La Butte	14	9AM	Proceeded to Reclinghem for Corps Practice	
Hpen	18	9AM	Proceeded to Ham in return for Corps Head	

Oms 2/24 T.M.B.y
N Divisn Heavy Bde.

WAR DIARY
or
INTELLIGENCE SUMMARY.
(Erase heading not required.)

Army Form C. 2118.

2ADAC   Vol 19   Sheet 1

Place	Date	Hour	Summary of Events and Information	Remarks and references to Appendices
Head Qrs MANQUE VILLE	Nov 1st		Weather fine, bright. One driver having joined from 21st D.A.C. proceeded to No 2 Sec. One driver from B Echelon having been transferred to Transport & Remount Depot struck off the strength. Supplied same fatigue party of 31 mounted men as yesterday & 106th Brigade.	RR
"	Nov 2nd		Weather cloudy & dull. Wind N. light. Same fatigue party supplied as yesterday.	RR
"	Nov 3rd		Weather mild & cold. Wind N. light. Supplied same mounted fatigue party.	RR
"	Nov 4th		Weather bright but cold. Wind S.E. light. Supplied 4 G.S. wagons to assist in moving Head Quarters D.A. from HAM-EN-ARTOIS to BETHUNE. Having received orders that Column to move on to Nos 1 & 2 Sections tomorrow and as B Echelon on the 6th inst. sent billeting party to HOUCHIN and VAUDRICOURT. During the past week ammunition was supplied to 106th & 107th Bdes for the purpose of calculating fires but as some part of this was returned at different intervals it was not possible to any event, the amount supplied. The ultimate result was as follows:- Originally supplied to Bdes	
			AX	BX
			900	600
			Returned by Bdes	415	403
			Nett amount supplied	485	197
			For the purpose of making good the deficiency caused by these supplies CAR had been on terms 300 AX & 400 BX the net result thus being to diminish ammunition on hand 13 X by 20 amount and nineteen 13X by 203 rounds.	

Army Form C. 2118.

WAR DIARY
or
INTELLIGENCE SUMMARY
(Erase heading not required.)

Sheet 2

Place	Date	Hour	Summary of Events and Information	Remarks and references to Appendices
Head Qrs HOUCHIN	Mch 5/15		Weather cold. Fall of snow commencing about 2.0 a.m. and lasting intermittently until 11 a.m.	
		8.0 a.m.	Head quarters + Nos 1 + 2 Section marched on full wheels from MANQUEVILLE LE CORNET BRASSART and LE CORNET BOURDOIS respectively to former billets at HOUCHIN. The ammunition 2nd Lt. H. BUGG having joined from 5-2nd Battery R.F.A. was posted to B Echelon 2nd Lt. G.L.T MADDISON was attached to Trench mortars 24th Divn. B Echelon (less 2.2 wagons away on fatigue at HERSIN) marched on full wheels from MANQUEVILLE to billets at VAUDRICOURT. Sent 25 G.S. wagon from here to MANQUEVILLE to transport the ammunition dumped there from the 22 wagons of B Echelon above referred to and the extra ammunition referred to under the entry of 4th instant. Weather fair but cold. Wind N. light.	app. 45. PP
	Mch 6th	7.	Weather dull, cold, Wind NE strong; frost at night :-	
"		8.	Lt. Wetzler posted to 106.18ᵈᵉ with effect from 6ᵗʰ. 2/Lt Meagher ordered to relieve Lieut Wetzler in Command of HERSIN group. Weather fine & snow showers. Wind NE fresh.	G.T.

WAR DIARY
or
INTELLIGENCE SUMMARY.

Army Form C. 2118.

Sheet 3

Place	Date	Hour	Summary of Events and Information	Remarks and references to Appendices
H⁴Q⁵	1917			
HOUCHIN Map 36 B	9ᵗʰ		Weather fine to Snow showers. Wind fresh E. Veering to S.E. and S.E. Warmer. 2.Lieut. J. C. Follett from D.A.C. on appointment and is posted to E.B. Echelon. Supplied working party of 1 Sergt. 1 Cpl. and 38 men for funeral of Canadian in S. of LORRETTE ridge. Map 36 B: to proceed on 10ᵗʰ inst.; Sent 1 N.C.O. and 20 men for Special work on T.M. emplacements, to BULLY GRENAY Map 36 B.	G.T.
	10ᵗʰ		Weather fine & still. Wind light S. Warmer. 2ⁿᵈ Lt. Davies and Working party returned. events Ł.S.B.O.Cy. Hants R.E's for work on emplacements to Column: 2 Lieut Mc Dewey returned from 1ˢᵗ Army School:-	G.T.
	11ᵗʰ		Weather fine & breezy. Wind light W. Supplied 20 G.S. Wagons with full teams for Divisional Artillery, to 12. Divisional R.E. Park and to Divisional Ammunition Col:- 7 p.s. Returning 2/Lt. Henry T.M. School Walking Wounded.	G.T.

WAR DIARY
INTELLIGENCE SUMMARY

Army Form C. 2118.
Sheet 4

Place	Date	Hour	Summary of Events and Information	Remarks and references to Appendices
	1917			
Head Qrs HOUCHIN	March 12th		Weather fine & dull and showery. Mules went Light W. Sent 3/Lt Denning out 2 Sergts 1 Cpl 55 O.Rs. 14.G.S. & 56 pack mules to Ngh Supply dump AIX NOULETTE. Sup. 36 B (R.22.a.4.) Supplied 3 G. G.S. wagons with food teams on various fatigues.	QT
"	13th		Weather fine clear wind light W. Supplied 17 G.S. wag. on ammunition and ration fatigues. 2/Lt Davis & party from attachment at HERSIN: B. Echelon moved from VAUDRICOURT to HESDIGNEUL	Sup 36 B & QT
"	14		Weather dull fine at first rain later. Received news that B. Echelon move to HESDIGNEUL from VAUDRICOURT. The clear of own fire at 2 pm to elay: Sent 1 Officer and 10 mem. G. R.21 A. 9.6 L. reinforce 2/Lieut Denning's party: Supplied 31 G.S wagons with food teams on ammunition transport and ration parties	QT Sup 36B
"	15		Weather fine dull clear direction NW moderate:- Supplied 33 G.S. wagons for transport of ammunition &c: sent 9. O.r.s. & T.M. battr to 17 division reinforcement arrived from base and post Hesdim —	QT

Army Form C. 2118.

Sheet 5

WAR DIARY
or
INTELLIGENCE SUMMARY.
(Erase heading not required.)

Place	Date	Hour	Summary of Events and Information	Remarks and references to Appendices
	1917			
HdQrs HOUCHIN	March 16		Weather fine. Wind Mod N. Cool & sunny. Supplied 27 G.S. Wagons with free trans for Ammunition Transport Work.	A.T.
	17		Weather fine, clear, bright sunshine. Wind graduate S.W. Warmer. Supplied 1st Div. Amn 14 G.S. Wagons for Ammunition Transport from VEDREL WOOD "Amn" Dump. To Gun positions near ABLAIN, St NAZAIRE	A.T.
	18		Fine dull at first, brighter later, with sunshine. Wind S.W. Light. Supplied 25 G.S. Wagons with full trans for transport of Ammunition. Commenced firing gun experiments S.R. units Ammunition.	A.T.
	19		Weather fine, cloudy, occasional bright periods. Wind S.W. Fresh to a gale later, with rain. Supplied 38 G.S. Wagons with full trans and 6 G.S. limbered wagons for Ammunition Transport.	A.T.

Army Form C. 2118.

Sheet 6

WAR DIARY
or
INTELLIGENCE SUMMARY
(Erase heading not required.)

Place	Date	Hour	Summary of Events and Information	Remarks and references to Appendices
	1917			
Head Qrs HOUCHIN	20 March		Weather fine cloudy. Wind strong W. Looking to N.W. and N. hail, sleet and snow showers. Coln. supplied 42 G.S. wagons with four teams for ammunition transport.	G.T.
	21 March		Weather fine. C.E.E. winds N. light. Supplied 46 G.S. wagons with four teams for ammunition transport. Detailed Lieut W. McKay as officer to superintend loading of gun ammunition of Royal Cdn. Arty. Lieut Humps in case of an advance and instructed him & N.C.O's himself acquainted with position of ammunition dumps at gun positions:-	G.T.
	22 March		Weather fine, cloudy with sight intervals. Snow showers during night 21-22". Wind Light N.E. Supplied 54 G.S. wagons with four teams for ammunition transport.	G.T.
	23"		Weather fine & snow showers Coln. Wind N.Light. Supplied 39 G.S. wagons with four teams for transport of ammunition.	G.T.

Army Form C. 2118.

WAR DIARY
or
INTELLIGENCE SUMMARY.
(Erase heading not required.)

Sheet 7

Place	Date	Hour	Summary of Events and Information	Remarks and references to Appendices
Head Qrs HOUCHIN	1917 June 24.		Weather fine clear. Wind NNE fresh. Supplied 27 G.S. wagons with pair teams and 2 G.S. limbered wagons for ammunition transport etc.	G.T.
	25"		Weather dull, fine occ'l wind NE cold. Wind backing to N-NW with some rain. Enemy shelled NOEUX LES MINES. Relieving duties during day. Supplied 40 G.S. wagons with pair teams for ammunition transport. The Devon Column & 2/Lt Scotty, Wounded light.	G.T.
	26"		Weather clear wet. Wind NW. Light. 41 O.Rs returned from work of instructing gun emplacements South of LORETTE RIDGE.	
	27		Weather dull occ'l some showers occasional bright intervals. Wind NE fresh. Supplied 63 G.S. wagons with pair teams for ammunition transport. 1/E.B. Rifleman moved from HESDIGNEUL to HOUCHIN.	G.T.
	28"		Weather fine cloudy with occasional some wind NW cold. Supplied 58 G.S. wagons for ammunition transport.	G.T.

Army Form C. 2118.
Sheet 8

WAR DIARY
INTELLIGENCE SUMMARY.
(Erase heading not required.)

Place	Date	Hour	Summary of Events and Information	Remarks and references to Appendices
	1917			
Head Qrs HOUCHIN	Mar 29		Weather wet, wind strong W: posted B.Gr. Lt. T.M.Batteries (A to Henry, 4 to Mervin Batteries) Enemy shelled NOEUX LES MINES from about 6.45pm to 7.45pm: supplied 75. G.S.Wagons for transport of Ammunition etc.	G.T.
	30.		Weather showery bright intervals wind strong W to N.W. 2nd Lieuts. D.H. Wallace T.F. A.W.Clark T.F. A.B.Longman T.F. 26pr and 2nd Lieut. 28 during joined from base. Enemy shelled NOEUX.LES. MINES from about 8.30am to 9.am. supplied 57 G.S. wagons for transport of Ammunition	G.T.
	31st		Weather showery. Bright intervals wind strong W to S.W. Supplied 42 G.S. Wagons for transport of Ammunition. Lieut. McKay + 2nd Lt. D.O.Weir, and 2 R horses 56 mules, 1 G.S. wagon and 76. O.R. returned from work in connection with Ammunition dumps. N of LORETTE RIDGE. Amount of Ammunition issued to group R.F.A. in March 1917.	G.T. Map 36 B.
			A AX BX	
			24,700 12,372 11,600	
			A = 18pr & J. Shrapnel: AX = 16pr QF. HE: BX = 4.5"How. HE.	
				G. Taunton Col. R.F.A. Comm'dg 24th D.A.C.
			March 31st 1917	

Army Form C. 2118.

WAR DIARY
or
INTELLIGENCE SUMMARY.
(Erase heading not required.)

Y24 TMB

Not

Instructions regarding War Diaries and Intelligence Summaries are contained in F.S. Regs., Part II. and the Staff Manual respectively. Title pages will be prepared in manuscript.

Place	Date	Hour	Summary of Events and Information	Remarks and references to Appendices
Calonne	1917. Nov 9-10	2 pm	Registered front line from M.20.b.5.4 to 9.5½ & support line from M.20.b.5½.2 to M.20.b.9.4½	
		10 am	Registered front line from M.15.b.8½.9¾ to M.15.d.9.6 & support line from M.16.a.4.8½ to M.16.a.1.5½	
	" 10-11	2-3 pm	Enemy front line & WIRE at M.20.b.5.4 M.20.b.5½.2 to M.20.b.9.4 on the latter case 10 incendiary bombs were used with good effect on three buildings	
		11 am	Retaliated on front line & support on M.20.6 & M.15.6.	
	11-12	9 am	Enemy front line & WIRE M.9.d.8.2 to M.15.6.9.6	
		2.30 pm	Enemy wire from M.20.6.9½.6½ to M.21.a.4.6	
		9 am	Enemy front line & WIRE from M.15.6.9.9 to M.15.6.9.6	
		10-15 am	Enemy wire from M.9.d.9.3 to M.9.d.8.0.	
	12-13	11 am	FOSSE 6 DE LENS M.10.0. & retaliation for 2 Enemy T.M.	
		3 pm	Registered enemy front & support lines on M.24.6.	
		9.30 am	Fired on enemy wire from M.15.6.9.9 to M.15.6.9.6	
	13-14	2.30 pm	Enemy wire from M.15.6.9.9.6	
		3.10 pm	Enemy wire & front line from M.14.d.6.6 to M.14.d.9.7½ Retaliation for Minnies	
		10.30 am	Enemy wire from M.15.6.9.9 to 9.6.	
	14-15	2 pm	Fired on Enemy wire M.15.6.9.9 to 9.6.	

2333 Wt. W:2344/1454 700,000 5/15 D.D.&L. A.D.S.S./Forms/C. 2118.

Army Form C. 2118.

WAR DIARY
or
INTELLIGENCE SUMMARY.
(Erase heading not required.)

Instructions regarding War Diaries and Intelligence Summaries are contained in F. S. Regs., Part II. and the Staff Manual respectively. Title pages will be prepared in manuscript.

Place	Date	Hour	Summary of Events and Information	Remarks and references to Appendices
Baloruri	1917 Nov			
	15-16	11 a.m.	Fired on enemy wire M.15 b.9.9. to 9.6.	
	16-17	12 midn.t	Fired on enemy front line from M.20 b.60.40 to M.21 a. 30.60.	
		10 a.m.	Fired on enemy wire from M.20 b.90.60 to M.21. a. 40.60	
	17-18	10 a.m.	Fired on enemy wire from M.21 b. 10.65 to M.21 d. 40.60.	
	18-19		Put guns in new emplacements	
		8-10 p.m.	Fired on enemy front line M.20 b S.52 to 56.42 to M.21.a. 32.52	
	19.20	12.30 p.	Fired on M.9.d.98.40 in cooperation with Artillery	
		5 pm	Fired on enemy wire between M.20 b. 90. 68 + M.21. a. 20.60.	
		10 a.m.	Fired on enemy front line M. 9 d. 98. 40.	
	20.21	2 p.m.	Fired on wire at M.20 b.90.68 to M.21a 20.60	
		5 "	do	
		11 "	do	
	21-22	2.30 p.	Fired on wire at M.20. b 90.68 to M.21.a. 20.60	
	22-3		Fired Gas bombs on house at M.21.a. 35.35 to M.20 d 80.20	
	23-24	3 p.m.	Fired on enemy wire between M.20.1.90.68 + M.21a 20.60	
		10 a.m.	ditto	

Army Form C. 2118.

WAR DIARY
or
INTELLIGENCE SUMMARY.

(Erase heading not required.)

Instructions regarding War Diaries and Intelligence Summaries are contained in F. S. Regs., Part II. and the Staff Manual respectively. Title pages will be prepared in manuscript.

Place	Date	Hour	Summary of Events and Information	Remarks and references to Appendices
Colonel	1917 Dec. 21-25	2 p.m.	Fired on enemy wire M.20.b.90.68 to M.21.a.20.60	
		3.15 p.	Fired on enemy wire M.15.b.82.99 to M.15.b.91.58	
		10 a.m.	Fired on enemy wire M.10.a.65.08 to M.10.b.45.98.	
	26.27	2.15 p.m.	Fired on wire at M.21.a.6.7	
		4 p.m.	Fired on wire at M.9.d.78-18	
		9 p.m.	Fired on trenches M.20.b.90.68 to M.21.a.20.60 Retaliation	
	28"		Fired 50 rds enemy wire at various points	
	29"		" 65 " on wire, front + outpost lines	
	30"		" 75 " on wire & M.G. Emplacement	
	31"		" 105 " on wire	
			" 110 " on wire.	

[signature] for O/C 1/24 7718.

Army Form C. 2118.

WAR DIARY
or
INTELLIGENCE SUMMARY.
(Erase heading not required.)

Z 24 T M B

Vol

Place	Date	Hour	Summary of Events and Information	Remarks and references to Appendices
Regina	7-3-17	6 p.	Battery relieved X/TC.	
	8-3-17		Too foggy owing to Infantry relief.	
	9-3-17			
	10-3-17	10.00 am	SPINNEY, RICHARD DEEP & SLAG HEAP guns registered on frontline.	
	11-3-17	10 am	BORAH gun registered on frontline trench.	
	12-3-17	10 am	Registered SLAG HEAP & RICHARD DEEP on wire.	
	13-3-17	2½ P.M.	Fired 47 rounds on wire. Tried new mixture at RICHARD DEEP.	
		5:3 p.	Wire cutting.	
	14-3-17			
	15-3-17		50 rds. on wire.	
	16-3-17		46 rds on wire.	

Army Form C. 2118.

WAR DIARY
or
INTELLIGENCE SUMMARY.
(Erase heading not required.)

Instructions regarding War Diaries and Intelligence
Summaries are contained in F. S. Regs., Part II.
and the Staff Manual respectively. Title pages
will be prepared in manuscript.

Place	Date	Hour	Summary of Events and Information	Remarks and references to Appendices
Nieppe	17-3-17		102 rds. wire cutting.	
"	18-3-17	10am	57 rds wire cutting.	
"	19-3-17		31 rds. wire cutting.	
"	20-3-17		Wire cutting.	
"	21-3-17		Wire cutting.	
"	22-3-17	8am	18 rds retaliation fr. H.T.M. near DORAN ALLEY. 30 rds fr. gun. Bombs fired on trench tramway sh.M 26 a 6.1.70 at 8.0 p.m.	
"	23-3-17	10.30am	16 rds retaliation fr H.T.M. & 77mm on DORAN ALLEY & PYRENEES.	
"	24-3-17	11.0am to 3.0p.m.	23 rds on wire.	
"	25-3-17		191 rds on wire.	
"	26-3-17		110 rds on wire. STUDD ALLEY gun reported on move.	
"	27-3-17		10 rds. cutting 79 rds	
"	28-3-17		10 rds - cutting 134 rds. Tanks & spotters reported SEAFORTH AP	
"	29-3-17		10 rds - cutting 50 rds	
"	30-3-17		10 rds cutting	
"	31-3-17		50 rds cutting	

Afternoon Patrol
O.C. Z/24

Army Form C. 2118.

WAR DIARY
or
INTELLIGENCE SUMMARY.

(Erase heading not required.)

Instructions regarding War Diaries and Intelligence Summaries are contained in F. S. Regs., Part II. and the Staff Manual respectively. Title pages will be prepared in manuscript.

Place	Date	Hour	Summary of Events and Information	Remarks and references to Appendices
HEZECQUES	1-5-17		Rest	
OUDEZEELE	10-5-17		"	
HALIFAX CAMP	18-5-17		"	
HILL ROAD	24-5-17		Bathing rehearsal x/12 3 T. M. B.	
"	25 "		Nil - nothing	
"	26 "			
"	27 "			
"	28 "			
"	29 "			
"	30 "			
"	31 "			

Thomas Toll Ra.
5/or 2/24 T. M. B.

2353 Wt. W3544/1454 700,000 5/15 D. D. & L. A.D.S.S./Forms/C. 2118.

TRENCH MORTAR BATTERIES

24th DIVISION

APRIL 1917

WAR DIARY or INTELLIGENCE SUMMARY

Army Form C. 2118.

X/24 T.M.B Vol 10

Place	Date	Hour	Summary of Events and Information	Remarks and references to Appendices
Souchez	April 1st		3 Guns in action. 47 Rounds fired at machine gun, which were causing annoyance to Infantry Patrols. Enemy very quiet. All guns laid on enemy wire and fortification orders, on enemy wire and trenches from S.2.D.40.16 to M.32.B.01.14. During June 10 Aug 591 rounds were fired. Observation was rather difficult, it being quite impossible to see some of the enemy wire. The front line being rained to the enemy wire. The front line being rather built at N°3 gun damaged at N°3 gun team built at fair, N° 24 gun emplacement demolished at M 82.c 61 and M.32. c.0.3. were hit at by action by German artillery fire. N° 4 gun was built at night 8 11/12th April 15 when N° 4 was again hit the two limits met N° 7 gun examined. N° 4 "D" in enemy trench at S.21.09 BC's to by examined constantly destroyed at hours being hit by enemy trenches completely destroyed at front line trench destroyed. Working Party. (Building anew wire fence.)	
	April 15th			

Army Form C. 2118.

WAR DIARY
or
INTELLIGENCE SUMMARY.
(Erase heading not required.)

Instructions regarding War Diaries and Intelligence Summaries are contained in F. S. Regs., Part II. and the Staff Manual respectively. Title pages will be prepared in manuscript.

Place	Date	Hour	Summary of Events and Information	Remarks and references to Appendices
	17th		Working Party (building road)	
	18		" "	
	19		— Working roads for Arriling	
	20		" "	
	21		" "	
	22		" "	
	23		Proceeded to Rest (HEZEAVES)	
	24			

F.E. Higgins Lieut RE
OC Y/24 TMB

2353 Wt. W2544/1454 700,000 5/15 D. D. & L. A.D.S.S./Forms/C. 2118.

Army Form C. 2118.

Y/24 TMB

WAR DIARY
or
~~INTELLIGENCE SUMMARY~~
(Erase heading not required.)

Place	Date	Hour	Summary of Events and Information	Remarks and references to Appendices
Calonne	1-4-17		Fired 112 rounds at Enemy Front Line & Supports in M.21.A.	
	2		Fired on Enemy Wire from M.20.B.5.5. to M.21.A.67. + from M.15.D.4.7. to M.15.B.9.8.	
	3		" M.20.B.8.5. to M.20.B.9.7.	
	4		" + front line from M.A.B.7.3. to M. + B.6.6. & in M.9.D.	
	5		— do — " M.9.D.9's.r. to M.9.D.8.0. & — M.10.C	
	6		— do — " — do — & 60 gas bombs in M.16.A.	
	7		— do — " M.15.B.6.3. to M.15.D.2.1.	
	8		— do — " M.21.A.1.7. to M.21.A.9.8.	
	9		— do — " M.15.B.60 to M.15.B.9.9.	
	10		— do — " + Support line in M.15.B. & M.15.D.	
	11		— do — " — do — M.H.C. & M.10.A.	
	12		— do — " — do — M.20.B.	
	13		Fired 10 rds. on Enemy front line. at 5.30 pm our daylight patrols reported that Enemy had evacuated his front system & Vincelles.	
	14		Bomber's party for 106" Pdr. RFA (building roads in front of LEVEN.)	
	15		— do — 106" Pdr. RFA.	

Army Form C. 2118.

WAR DIARY
or
INTELLIGENCE SUMMARY

(Erase heading not required.)

Instructions regarding War Diaries and Intelligence Summaries are contained in F. S. Regs., Part II. and the Staff Manual respectively. Title pages will be prepared in manuscript.

Place	Date	Hour	Summary of Events and Information	Remarks and references to Appendices
	16.4.17		Working party for 106th Bde. R.F.A. building roads for artillery.	
	17.4.17		— do — and salvaging bombs in Balone & Maroc section.	
	18.4.17		Working party. Making roads for Artillery. Salvaging bombs.	
	19.4.17		— do — — do —	
	20.4.17		— do — — do —	
	21.4.17		Carrying party for 7/24 in Lieven.	
	22.4.17			
	23.4.17			
HEZECQUES.	24.4.17		Proceeded to GHQ.	

A. Menneth Lieut. R.F.A.
O.C. 7/24 T.M.Bty.

Army Form C. 2118.

Z/24 T MB

WAR DIARY
or
INTELLIGENCE SUMMARY.
(Erase heading not required.)

Instructions regarding War Diaries and Intelligence Summaries are contained in F. S. Regs., Part II. and the Staff Manual respectively. Title pages will be prepared in manuscript.

Place	Date	Hour	Summary of Events and Information	Remarks and references to Appendices
Augres	Sept 1-4-17	—	5.5 rds on mine.	
—	2-4-17	—	Wire cutting	
—	3-4-17	—	70 rds on wire & front line	
	4-			
	5-			
	6-			
	7-			
	8-			
	9-			
	10-			
	11-			
	12-			
—	13-4-17	—	Good return fire when of our front Battery unsupported and taken.	
Cité Calonne	14-4-17	—	Guns withdrawn from line to type in CITÉ CALONNE	
	15-	—	Guns in readiness to go into action at short notice	
	16	—	Fired 20 rounds of Shrapnel to forward position in Liévin	

Army Form C. 2118.

WAR DIARY
or
INTELLIGENCE SUMMARY.
(Erase heading not required.)

Instructions regarding War Diaries and Intelligence Summaries are contained in F. S. Regs., Part II. and the Staff Manual respectively. Title pages will be prepared in manuscript.

Place	Date	Hour	Summary of Events and Information	Remarks and references to Appendices
City about	17	—	Brought up 30 rounds to advance forward to	
"	18			
"	19	—	Brought up 30 rounds to advance further in line	
"	20	3 p.m.	11 casualties forwards in front of Loos	
	21			
2ª	22	R	Put in Guns in front of Loos in M.24.c.58.70.	
	22		awaiting orders	
	23	9.15	Started firing with artillery in front 119 more through the night to the movement forward of the Division	
	24		Relieved	
	25		Went to Rest camp	
	26			
	27			
	28			
	29			
	30			

Stolinien Group F.A.
S.C. Z/24 T.M.B.

WAR DIARY
or
INTELLIGENCE SUMMARY.

(Erase heading not required.)

Army Form C. 2118.

Instructions regarding War Diaries and Intelligence Summaries are contained in F. S. Regs., Part II. and the Staff Manual respectively. Title pages will be prepared in manuscript.

Place	Date	Hour	Summary of Events and Information	Remarks and references to Appendices
HAZEBROUCK	1/7/15			
— do —	9/7/15			
HAZEBROUCK	10/7/15		— do —	
OUDEZEELE	11/7			
ZILLEBEKE	24/7		Trench Cur position near LARCH WOOD & Railway Cutting I.29.c.	
	25/7		— do —	
	26/7		— do —	
	27/7		— do —	
	28/7		— do —	
	29/7		Hel 42.1k or Enemy from line from I.34. A.66 to I.29 D.1.k	
	30/7		— do — + Mines	
	31/7		— do —	

V/24 H.T.M. 13

WAR DIARY
or
INTELLIGENCE SUMMARY.

Army Form C. 2118.

24 D T M By

Vol XI

Place	Date May	Hour	Summary of Events and Information	Remarks and references to Appendices
Hill 60	25th	8.P.M.	Took over gun partly made gun position from V/23. Bde in very bad condition. Pivoted & full round	
"	26th		Pumped out No 2 Pit got some of the mud out, And one gun sent up to Jackson's Dump	
"	27th		Unable to do any work except keep No 2 Pit pumped out & moved gun from bump steengly shelled all day. S.O.S. 11:15 A.M.	
"	28th		Put gun in No3 Position that his more guns up to Jackson's Dump	
"	29th		making Gun Positions	
"	30		"	
"	31		"	

Army Form C. 2118.

WAR DIARY
or
INTELLIGENCE SUMMARY.
(Erase heading not required.)

Instructions regarding War Diaries and Intelligence Summaries are contained in F. S. Regs., Part II. and the Staff Manual respectively. Title pages will be prepared in manuscript.

Vol 12
Dimensional Trench Mortar Battería on D.A.

Place	Date	Hour	Summary of Events and Information	Remarks and references to Appendices
Afgned	1914			
	1st June		Found 110 rds Front line & wire I.29.c	
	2"		" 123 " Front & Support line & Crater I.29.c+D	
	3"		" 25 " Support line & Crater wire I.29.c+D	
	4"		" 40 " Ditto Ditto	
	5"		" 59 " Support line Wire I.29.d	
	6"		" 37 " Front line & Crater Wire & Support line I.29.d	
	21/6/16 2/6/		No firing	
	22d		Fired 25 rds Front line & Supports I.25.a & I.30.b	
	23d		" 20 " T.25.a.6.6 to T.25.a.58.88	
	24th		" 37 " Front line Supports I.25.a+B	
	25th		" 40 " Ditto Ditto	
	26th		" 14 " on T.30.b & T.25.a.25.95	
	27th		" 25 " Front line T.30.b	
	30th		" 20 " on T.25.A	
	29th		" 23 " on T.30.b & T.25.A	

Army Form C. 2118.

WAR DIARY
or
INTELLIGENCE SUMMARY.

(Erase heading not required.)

Place	Date	Hour	Summary of Events and Information	Remarks and references to Appendices
Tiffains	1917 30 June		Ypres 25 rds on Wood Line T.30.b. + Dugouts at T.25.a 58 88	

H Thoms Capt RFA
O/C 7710 am RDB

Instructions regarding War Diaries and Intelligence Summaries are contained in F. S. Regs., Part II. and the Staff Manual respectively. Title pages will be prepared in manuscript.

WAR DIARY
or
INTELLIGENCE SUMMARY.
(Erase heading not required.)

Army Form C. 2118.

Divisional Trench Mortar Batteries
24th Divisional Artillery

Vol 13

Place	Date	Hour	Summary of Events and Information	Remarks and references to Appendices
	1917			
Ypres	1 July		Fired 40 rds on Enemy support line at I.19.c.	
	2		" 66 " on Enemy support & front line at J.20.b.	
	3		" 20 " on do do	
	4		Relieved by 23rd Divisional T. M. Batteries	
[illegible]	5th to 14th		At Rest	
Ypres	15th		Took over old position	
	16th		Working parties & carrying parties	
	17th		do do	
	18th		Relieved 23rd Divl T. M. Batteries in the line.	
	19th		Working on positions	
	20th		Ditto	
	21st		Ditto	
	22nd		Fired 70 rounds on support line at I.25.a.55.70. New 6" Newton Mortar used.	
	23rd		" 50 " on Hedge Support at I.25.a.4.45.	
	24th		" 63 " on [illegible] in J.25.a.	

2353 Wt. W2544/1454 700,000 5/15 D. D. & L. A.D.S.S./Forms/C. 2118.

Army Form C. 2118.

WAR DIARY
or
INTELLIGENCE SUMMARY.
(Erase heading not required.)

Instructions regarding War Diaries and Intelligence Summaries are contained in F. S. Regs., Part II. and the Staff Manual respectively. Title pages will be prepared in manuscript.

Place	Date	Hour	Summary of Events and Information	Remarks and references to Appendices
	10/4			
	23/6		Last shown at T.25 c.25, 25.25. Range of T.25 central shown by figures	
			T.25.D.0.4 + Northerns - Range shown by figures	
	26		16 shelling	
			" " shew shoots	
	27		26 " "	
	28		57 " T.25 d. 1.30.10 + flash [?]	
	29		11 " Battalion [?] searchlights traveller [?]	
	30		30 " ditto ditto	
	31		63 " ditto ditto	
			All available Officers and men acted as available bearers at Dressing Station	

2353 Wt. W2544/1454 700,000 5/15 D. D. & L. A.D.S.S./Forms/C. 2118.

Army Form C. 2118.

WAR DIARY
INTELLIGENCE SUMMARY.
77th Divisional Trench Mortar Batteries

(Erase heading not required.)

Vol / 4

Instructions regarding War Diaries and Intelligence Summaries are contained in F. S. Regs., Part II. and the Staff Manual respectively. Title pages will be prepared in manuscript.

Place	Date	Hour	Summary of Events and Information	Remarks and references to Appendices
Officers	1917			
	1 Aug	Fired out		
	2d	do do		
	3d		All available officers & men engaged as stretcher bearers.	
	4th		Ditto. No. 99969 Cpl. H. Lord & No. 57492 Pte. W. Coles Bde. awarded Military Medal.	
	5th	Fired out		
	6th		N.C.O. & 6 men engaged at Artillery Headquarters on fatigue	
	7th	do do		
	8th	do do		
	9th	do do		
	10th	do do		
	11th		N.C.O. & 21 o.r. engaged in carrying ammunition &c	
	12th	ditto	ditto	
	13th	2 N.C.O. & 48 men	ditto	
	14th	ditto	ditto	
	15th	ditto	ditto	
	16th	ditto	Relieved 233 T.M.B. on the line - Removed from line 12 · 2 · M.	
	17th	ditto	ditto	

Army Form C. 2118.

WAR DIARY
or
INTELLIGENCE SUMMARY.
(Erase heading not required.)

Instructions regarding War Diaries and Intelligence Summaries are contained in F. S. Regs., Part II. and the Staff Manual respectively. Title pages will be prepared in manuscript.

Place	Date	Hour	Summary of Events and Information	Remarks and references to Appendices
Dijon	17 Aug		All available N.C.Os. & men engaged on sorting & movement etc.	
	18"		Ditto	
	19"		Ditto	
	20"		Ditto	
	21"		Ditto	
	22"		Ditto	
	23"		Ditto	
	24"		Ditto	
	25"		Two Officers & all available N.C.O. & men	
	26"		Ditto	
	27"		Ditto	
	28"		Ditto	
	29"		1 Officer & all available N.C.Os. & men	Handed q. n.5 (Reg.) 7th from line.
	30"		ditto	
	31"		ditto	

Army Form C. 2118.

WAR DIARY
or
INTELLIGENCE SUMMARY

(Erase heading not required.)

24 Div T.M.B.

Sept. 1917

Vol 15

Army Form C. 2118.

WAR DIARY
OR
INTELLIGENCE SUMMARY. 2nd Divisional Trench Mortar Battery
(Erase heading not required.)

Place	Date	Hour	Summary of Events and Information	Remarks and references to Appendices
Officers	1 Feb		M. available N.C.O. & men engaged on taking ammunition	
	2"		Removed guns from the line	
	3"		Shelter huts engaged on making emplacement	
	4"		Ditto	
	5"		Ditto	
	6"		Ditto	
	7"		2 Officers 50 men engaged on Gun pit digging	
	8"		1 Officer 25 men Ditto Ditto	
	9"		Ditto	
	10"		Ditto	
	11"		Ditto	
	12"		Handed over 2 6" Newton T.M. to D.T.M.O. 23rd D.A. Fatigue party relieved	
	13th		Handed over 1 9.45 T.M. to D.T.M.O. 39th D.A.	
	14"		First stages of journey to new area - Owned Steenvoorde	
Steenvoorde	15"		Preparation for entrainment	
do	16"		Ditto	

Army Form C. 2118.

WAR DIARY
or
INTELLIGENCE SUMMARY.
(Erase heading not required.)

Instructions regarding War Diaries and Intelligence Summaries are contained in F.S. Regs., Part II. and the Staff Manual respectively. Title pages will be prepared in manuscript.

Place	Date	Hour	Summary of Events and Information	Remarks and references to Appendices
BAPAUME	1917 17/10		Entrained for rest area	
"	18th		Arrived at BAPAUME 3.10 a.m.	
"	19th		In Rest Camp	
"	20th		Ditto. Inspection by C.R.A.	
"	21st		Ditto	
"	22nd		Ditto	
"	23rd		Ditto	
"	24th		Ditto	
DOINGT	25th		Moved to DOINGT	
"	26th		At DOINGT	
"	27th		D.T.M.O. proceeded to forward area to reconnoitre, remaining at Hermily	
"	28th		Batteries at DOINGT	
HERMILY	29th		Batteries moved to forward area arriving at destination at 13 hrs.	
	30th		Relieved 24th T.M.B. in the line	

2353 Wt. W3541/1454 700,000 5/15 D. D. & L. A.D.S.S./Forms/C. 2118.

Confidential

9/II 16

War Diary for month of October 1917

of 24th D.T.M.O.

Army Form C. 2118.

WAR DIARY
—or—
INTELLIGENCE SUMMARY.
(Erase heading not required.)

24th Divisional Trench Mortar Battery

Place	Date	Hour	Summary of Events and Information	Remarks and references to Appendices
HERVILLY	1917 Oct 1		Ammunition expended Nil. - Personnel engaged building dugouts & gun pit detachments	
	2		Ditto	
	3		One officer & 18 other ranks proceeded to Wood Post 77A to lay track on road	
	4		Do	
	5		Ammunition expended nil - Work on dugouts continued	
	6		Construction of 6" Newton TM emplacement.	
	6		Personnel relieved from 77A Post 77A.	
	7		Stokes battery fired 5 ros Registration	
	8		Do 6. Do Do. Ditto Retaliation	
	9		Do 4 Do Do. - good effect obtained.	
	10		Do 7 ros Registration - Medium battery engaged in harassing	
	10		Ammunition expended NB. - Work on trenches continued.	
			Lt. Registration Ditto	
	11		" do Ditto	
	12		" " Ditto	
	13		" 5 ros	
	14			
	15		Heavy Battery fired 11 ros Offensive & Registration - Medium Bttn engaged on work on positions & dugouts	
	16		Ammunition expended Nil. Ditto	

Army Form C. 2118.

WAR DIARY
or
INTELLIGENCE SUMMARY.

(Erase heading not required.)

Instructions regarding War Diaries and Intelligence Summaries are contained in F. S. Regs., Part II. and the Staff Manual respectively. Title pages will be prepared in manuscript.

Place	Date	Hour	Summary of Events and Information	Remarks and references to Appendices
HERVILLY	1917 Oct 17		Medium R.B fired 18 rds on G.2.c.30.70. Heavy guns out of action - prevented searching, repair	
	18		" " 26 " G.8.d.00.35. Do	
	19		Ammunition expended Nil. Men engaged building foodline & dugout	
	20		Do Do Do	
	21		Do Do Do	
	22		Medium R.B fired 12 rds on G.2.c.15.50 - G.1.a.95.15. Dried kit & Marest	
	23		Ammunition expended Nil. Work of construction continued	
	24		Do Do	
	25		Medium R.B fired 12 rds on TRENCH at G.2.c.6.9. Heavy Stg Mort fired 2 rds on G.2.d.1.6. Looking upon hole	
	26		Ammunition expended 11 brds. Work of construction with road	
	27		Heavy Trench fired 10 rds on G.2.b.10.66.	
	28		Medium 9.5 fired 5 rds on G.2.a.4.4.	
	30		Ammunition expended Nil. Work continued on dugout	
	30		Ammunition expended 3 rds on enemy wire & trenches - 1.9 m/m handed over to 2nd Div	
	31		Ammunition expended 18 rds on enemy MM & 4 fired at front G.2.c.15.90 - 25.75.	

H. Thomas ????
for ?? ?? ?? ???

SECRET.

15

Vol 17

War Diary

24th Divisional Trench Mortar Batteries

from Nov 1st to Nov 30th

1917

Army Form C. 2118.

WAR DIARY
or
INTELLIGENCE SUMMARY
(Erase heading not required.)

24th Division / See A. Andre Bottrall

Instructions regarding War Diaries and Intelligence Summaries are contained in F. S. Regs., Part II and the Staff Manual respectively. Title pages will be prepared in manuscript.

Place	Date	Hour	Summary of Events and Information	Remarks and references to Appendices
HERMIES	1917 1st Nov.		Medium Howrs fired 31 rds on enemy area from G.9.C.15.98 - 20.91 & wirecutting at G.h.d 90.25.	
			Shooting very effective.	
			Heavy Battery fired 4 rds on A.26.d.1.11 in retaliation.	
	2nd "		Medium Howrs fired O rds on wire v Junction G.2.C.10.05 - 20.16. Explosion and enemy fired.	
			Heavy Battery fired 5 rds registering G.3.a.60.10	
	3rd "		Medium Battery fired 62 rds on transport & trenches. Who shot was very effective	
			Heavy Battery fired 6 rds on G.2.a.60.0	
			Heavy Battery fired 9 rds registering G.2.C.58. Medium Battery engaged medium 76.74 howitzer	
	4th "		Guns observed on nr. ducking positions.	
	5th "		Medium Battery fired 36 rds identification G.21.a.82.83 in retaliation	
	6th "		Medium Howrs fired 6 rds on enemy parties & dugouts. Band to channel	
	7th "		Medium Battery fired 2 rds on enemy dugouts at G.2.C. 72.75. Nil observed.	
	8th "		Medium Battery fired 12 rds on enemy batteries at G.2.C.32.82 & A.26.d.3.5.	
	9th "		Medium Battery fired 33 rds on heavy Trench Mortar & dugouts. Band 250 Rounds	
	10th "		Heavy Battery fired 8 rds on G.2.A.70 in retaliation	
	11th "		Medium Battery fired 5 rds on SNOY TRENCH in retaliation	

Army Form C. 2118.

WAR DIARY
or
INTELLIGENCE SUMMARY.
(Erase heading not required.)

Instructions regarding War Diaries and Intelligence Summaries are contained in F. S. Regs., Part II. and the Staff Manual respectively. Title pages will be prepared in manuscript.

Place	Date	Hour	Summary of Events and Information	Remarks and references to Appendices
	11th		Nothing to report. 25 rds on enemy zone. Very effective.	
	12th		Intern Balloon. Fired 3rds on enemy zone — Gas made.	
	13th		Enemy Battery had broken C.2.d 45 rds × G.2.d.25.32 unretaliated	
	14th		Nothing. Balloon fired 10 rds on enemy — Effective shooting & gas made	
	15th		Enemy Battery positions at C.2.a.92.35 & G.2.b.1.10 counterbattered	
			Nothing. Batteries fired 60 rds on zone — Infantry signal large gas made	
	16th		Nothing. Balloon zone 28 rds on enemy point	
			Enemy Battery fired 15d on retaliation	
	17th		Nothing. Balloon fired 50 rds on enemy "hostile" zone. Enemy shore shelled	
			Intern Balloon fired 36 rds on Enemy zone — No retaliation unused any shells	
			Enemy Battery fired 3 rds registering G.2.1.6.3.92	
	19th		Nothing. Balloon fired 116 rds on enemy front line dugouts — Enemy effective shelling	
			shelled road 116 rds on enemy lines — Very heavy uncut line	
			large quantity of mud was seen flew the enemy making no	
	20th		Nothing. Battery fired 88 rds reg. along roads in enemy's quarters & on a gun emplacement	
	21st		Nothing. Battery fired 1465 rds on counter battery work and — Very heavy uncut heavy	
			without being able to spot at any point.	

24th Divisional Trench Mortar Batteries

Confidential

War Diary for the month of December 1917

Army Form C. 2118.

WAR DIARY
or
INTELLIGENCE SUMMARY.

(Erase heading not required.)

14th Divisional Trench Mortar Battery

Instructions regarding War Diaries and Intelligence Summaries are contained in F. S. Regs., Part II. and the Staff Manual respectively. Title pages will be prepared in manuscript.

Place	Date	Hour	Summary of Events and Information	Remarks and references to Appendices
HARGICOURT.	1917. 1 Dec		Personnel engaged on repairing damaged gun positions	
	2"		Medium Batteries fired 325 rds on selected targets in conjunction with usual programme of Arty.	
			Heavy Battery fired 11 rds. Ditto	
	3"		Medium Batteries fired 180 rds on selected targets.	
			Heavy Battery fired 9 rds. ditto & 3 rounds checking registration of G.2.c.5.1.	
	4"		Medium Batteries fired 33 rds on Trench Junction KILDARE & WOOD TRENCH on Hargicourt	
			Heavy Battery fired 5 rds on A.26.b.30.15 registration.	
	5"		Medium Batteries fired 18 rds on Machine gun positions at G.2.a.7.1	
	6"		Medium Batteries fired 224 rds on selected targets in special demonstration	
			Heavy Battery fired 10 rds. ditto ditto.	
	7"		Medium Batteries fired 400 rds in wire cutting for raid. Large gap made in wire.	
	8"		Medium Batteries fired 372 rds on selected targets in support of raid.	
			Heavy Battery fired 22 rds. ditto	
	9"		Personnel engaged on constructing positions	
	10"		Medium Batteries fired 41 rds on trench junction at G.2.c.6.3 & M.G. emplacement at G.2.a.2.2"	
			Heavy Battery fired 11 rds on QUENNEMONT FARM.	

Army Form C. 2118.

WAR DIARY
or
INTELLIGENCE SUMMARY.
(Erase heading not required.)

Instructions regarding War Diaries and Intelligence Summaries are contained in F. S. Regs., Part II. and the Staff Manual respectively. Title pages will be prepared in manuscript.

Place	Date	Hour	Summary of Events and Information	Remarks and references to Appendices
	11th		Medium Batteries fired 135 rds on trench junctions & dugouts in rear of first	
	12th		Medium Batteries fired 118 rds on wire in front of RUBY WOOD as G.S.C. 20.15 - special programme	
	13th		Medium Batteries fired 131 rds on selected targets for special operation.	
	14th		Personal registration on damaged positions - casualty rnds attached.	
	15th		Ditto	
	16th		Medium Batteries fired 100 rds on enemy trenches & trench junctions on organised hostile batteries	
	17th		Heavy Battery fired 5 rds registering hostile Bn. at A.26.A.8.6. Personnel engaged on rifle & Lewis gun dummy posture covering hostile carrying parties & escorting cavalry Trs.	
	18th		Ditto }	
	19th		Ditto } Firing Nil owing to snow	
	20th		Ditto }	
	21st		Ditto }	
	22nd		Ditto }	
	23rd		Ditto	
	24th		Medium Batteries fired 120 rds on selected targets on special artillery programme	

Army Form C. 2118.

WAR DIARY
or
INTELLIGENCE SUMMARY. Continuation

(Erase heading not required.)

Place	Date	Hour	Summary of Events and Information	Remarks and references to Appendices
	24th		Heavy Howitzer fired 3rds on hostile Tr at A 25 A S 6.	
	25th		Personnel engaged on positions in the line.	
	26th		ditto. Preparations for removing German hut from number at I.1.a.70.10	
	27th		ditto ditto	
	28th		ditto ditto	
	29th		ditto ditto	
	30th		ditto ditto	
	31st		ditto ditto	

Army Form C. 2118.

WAR DIARY

(Erase heading not required.)

X/24 TMB

Vol #7

Place	Date	Hour	Summary of Events and Information	Remarks and references to Appendices
Loos	1-1-17		Fired 5 Rounds on Enemy Supports & Harassing	
"	2d		" 25 " " Wire Cutting	
"	3d		" 41 " " Wire Cutting	
"	4d		" 38 " " Retaliation, RBM's give trouble	
"	5d		" 59 " " Enemy Wire constructing new position	
"	6d		" 37 " " Still working on new emplacement	
"	7d		" 47 " " Preparation for future operation	
"	8d		" 69 " " Wire still being carried on in new emplacement	
"	9d		" 25 " " Wire Cutting	
"	10d		" 24 " " "	
"	11d		" 2 " " to armoury yd for rest	
"	12d		" 14 " " Completed new emplacement, registered same	
"	13d		" 36 " " Offensive	
"	14d		" 94 " " Enemy Supports	
"	15d		" 49 " " Lotes trouble in L.d.R Pt	
"	16d		" 45 " " Enemy Supports & Harassive, assumed full short	

Army Form C. 2118.

X/24 T M B

WAR DIARY
or
~~INTELLIGENCE SUMMARY~~
(Erase heading not required.)

Instructions regarding War Diaries and Intelligence Summaries are contained in F. S. Regs., Part II. and the Staff Manual respectively. Title pages will be prepared in manuscript.

Place	Date	Hour	Summary of Events and Information	Remarks and references to Appendices
Loos	July 17		Quiet 10 Rounds on TM Emplacement, good results	
"	18		22 " " wire cutting	
"	19		10 " " Enemy supports & cutting wire	
"	20		51 " " Wire cutting round junction, fair shift very good results	
"	21		90 " " Enemy front line & supports many direct hits	
"	22		20 " " Supports	
"	23		36 " " Enemy supports & Hanover	
"	24		38 " " Enemy front line several good modern Hanover	
"	25		3 " " Enemy supports	
"	26		25 " " Supports at M.G.C	
"	27		12 " "	
"	28		Nil " "	
"	29		30 " " Reformed trenches & gun pits	
"	30		35 " " Enemy fire line & Hanover	
"	31		15 " " "	

P.S. Higgins Lieut RFA
O.C. X/24 TMB

X/24 T.M.B.

Army Form C. 2118.

WAR DIARY
or
INTELLIGENCE SUMMARY.
(Erase heading not required.)

Vol 8. Sheet 1

Place	Date	Hour	Summary of Events and Information	Remarks and references to Appendices
Loos	1-2-17		Fired 90 rounds on enemy Support lines	
	2"		" 45 " Support	
	3"		" 49 " Support M.G.C.	
	4"		" 20 " Support M.50 + D.	
	5"		" 23 " Support	
	6"		" 35 " Support (night firing)	
	7"		" 24 " Front line & Supports	
	8"		" 53 " Front line & Supports (night firing)	
	9"		" 14 " Wire & Front line	
	10"		" 3 " Wire & Front line	
	11"		" 17 " Front line	
	12"		Nil	
	13th		Handed over to X/137 T.M.B.	
Nipwid	14-M-17	11.65.am	Proceeded to Lestrem for Divisional Rest	
			At LESTREM	
	18		Moved to HAM. EN. ARTOIS.	

Army Form C. 2118.

Sheet 2

WAR DIARY
or
INTELLIGENCE SUMMARY.
(Erase heading not required.)

Instructions regarding War Diaries and Intelligence Summaries are contained in F. S. Regs., Part II. and the Staff Manual respectively. Title pages will be prepared in manuscript.

Place	Date	Hour	Summary of Events and Information	Remarks and references to Appendices
HAM EN ARTOIS 28th.4.16 (2am)			Divisional Rest	

L.P. Higgins Lieut.
O/c X/24 TMB

Sheet No. 1.

Army Form C. 2118.

X 24 T M B

Vol 9

WAR DIARY

INTELLIGENCE SUMMARY

(Erase heading not required.)

Instructions regarding War Diaries and Intelligence Summaries are contained in F. S. Regs., Part II. and the Staff Manual respectively. Title pages will be prepared in manuscript.

Place	Date	Hour	Summary of Events and Information	Remarks and references to Appendices
	1917			
	12 March	12.45 pm	2 rounds on S2.b.20.40 to S2.b.60.20. (German front line)	
	"	1.15 pm	2 " "	} In retaliation.
	"	1.45 pm	2 " "	
	"	2.30 "	2 " "	
	"	3.0 "	2 " S2.b.70.40 to S2.b.70.20 (German support line).	
	"	3.30 "	2 " "	
	14 March	11.45 am	14 rounds on enfilade post at S2.b.30.40. and S2.b.65.15.	
	16 March	10.30 "	20 " " S2.b.20.40 to S2.b.60.20.	(1)
	"	10.30 "	12 " " M32.d.10.30.15 M32.d.40.20	(2)
	"	10.30 "	2 " " M32.d.40.20 to S2.b.40.90. (German Front line).	(3)
	17 "	11 am	15 " } Targets as above	(1)
	"	11 am	15 "	(2)
	"	11 am	15 "	(3)
	19 "	3 pm	3 " S2.b.20.40 to S2.b.60.20. (F.L.T.)	
	"	3 pm	20 " S.L. and rain at S2.b.65.82.	
	"	10.30 pm	10 " S2.b.20.40 to S2.b.60.20 (F.L.T) (Retaliation for minenwerfer).	

(Continued on Sheet No. 2)

Sheet No 2
Army Form C. 2118.

WAR DIARY
or
INTELLIGENCE SUMMARY

(Erase heading not required.)

Instructions regarding War Diaries and Intelligence Summaries are contained in F. S. Regs., Part II. and the Staff Manual respectively. Title pages will be prepared in manuscript.

(Continued on Sheet No 3)

Place	Date	Hour	Summary of Events and Information	Remarks and references to Appendices
	1917		Sirwuda on	
	March 22	10.30am	F.L at S.28 & 0.35. (Retaliation)	
		2.00pm	Sirwuda on banks at S.26 50.25. & S.2 & 60.15.	R.B.M onward after 18th round
		2.30pm	15 rounds on wire from M.32 d 50.00 to S.2 a 32.52.	" " " " 16th "
	" 23	11.30am	5 " " F.L at S.2 & 25.35.	" " " " 16th "
		6.20pm	5 " " "	
		1.30 "	5 " " F.L at M.32 d 20.30.	
		2.30 "	5 " "	
		11.30am	6 " " M.32d 20.10 to S.2 & 40.90. (F.L.T.)	
		3.15pm	3 " "	
	" 23	10.15am	15 Target (1) as on March 16	
		10.45am	10:15:10	
		3.0pm		
		11.0am	15 rounds Target as (2) on March 16	
		12 noon		
		7.30pm		

2353 Wt W3544/1454 700,000 5/15 D.D.&L. A.D.S.S./Forms/C.2118.

Sheet No 3.
Army Form C. 2118.

WAR DIARY
or
INTELLIGENCE SUMMARY
(Erase heading not required.)

Instructions regarding War Diaries and Intelligence Summaries are contained in F. S. Regs., Part II. and the Staff Manual respectively. Title pages will be prepared in manuscript.

Place	Date	Hour	Summary of Events and Information	Remarks and references to Appendices
	1917			
	March 23 (cont)	11am	4 rounds on ⎱	
		6.30pm	" ⎰ Jargelon (3) on March 16.	
		9.15 "	"	
		10.15pm	6 " ⎱	
	March 24	7am	5 " ⎰ S28.a.0.40 to S28.60.20 (F.L.T)	
		1.00am	5 "	
		9am	5 " ⎱	
		1pm	5 " ⎰ M32d 10.30 to M32d 40.20 (F.L.T)	
		2pm	6 " ⎱	
		4.30pm	6 " ⎰ M32d 40.20 to S28 65.90. (S.L.)	
	" 25	1pm	5 " ⎱	
		4.30pm	5 " ⎰ F.L.T & Wire M.32 d20.10 to S2.6.a.90.	
	" 26	5.15pm	7 " M32d 40.20 to S2 & 65 90 (S.L.).	
	" 27	6.30pm	7 " F.L.T & Wire M.32 d10.30 to M32d 40.20.	
		1pm	6 " ⎱	
		4pm	4 " ⎰ F.L.T & Wire M32d 20.10 to S2.6.40.90	

(Concluded on Sheet No 4)

Sheet No. 1.

Army Form C. 2118.

WAR DIARY
or
INTELLIGENCE SUMMARY.
(Erase heading not required.)

Instructions regarding War Diaries and Intelligence Summaries are contained in F. S. Regs., Part II. and the Staff Manual respectively. Title pages will be prepared in manuscript.

Place	Date	Hour	Summary of Events and Information	Remarks and references to Appendices
	Mar 28	4.15pm	5 rounds on F.L. O Wire S2 d 10.30 to M32 d 40.20.	
		11.00am	10 " M32 d 40.20 to S2 d 65.90. (S.L.)	
		5.0pm	10 " M32 d 20.10 to S2 d 40.90. (F L O Wire)	
		6.0pm	4 " "	
	29	11am	16 " German Wire M32 a 80.85 to M32 d 00.60.	
		2pm	5 " M32 d 10.30 to M32 d 40.20. (F.L.T)	
		3pm	5 " M32 d 20.10 to S2 d 40.90. (F L O Wire).	
		10am	5 " M32 d 00.30 (German M.G.)	
	30	10.30am	6 " M32 d 12.18 to S2 d 40.90 (F.L.T)	
		3pm	7 " M32 d 00.30 (German M.G.)	
		3.30pm	6 " M32 d 12.18 to S2 d 40.90 (F.L.T.)	
	31	10.30am	4 " M32 d 12.22 (S.L)	
		11am	5 " M32 d 16.14. (F.L.T.)	
		3pm	10 " "	
		3.30pm	15 " M32 d 12.22 (S.L.)	

W. Bottomley
Lieut
fo O.C. X/24. T.M.B.

Army Form C. 2118.

X/24 T.M.B.

WAR DIARY
or
INTELLIGENCE SUMMARY.
(Erase heading not required.)

Instructions regarding War Diaries and Intelligence Summaries are contained in F. S. Regs., Part II. and the Staff Manual respectively. Title pages will be prepared in manuscript.

Place	Date	Hour	Summary of Events and Information	Remarks and references to Appendices
HEZECOURS	1-9-17		REST	
OUDEZEELE	10-5-17			
HALIFAX CAMP	18-5-17			
HILL 60	23-5-17		BATTERY RELIEVED 2/23 T.M.B. WIRE CUTTING. A LINE & SUPPORTS	
"	26			
"	27			
"	28			
"	29			
"	30			
"	31			

L.S. Higgins
O.C. X/24 T.M.B.
X/24 T.M.B

T.M. 19

24th. Divisional Trench Mortar Batteries

Confidential

War Diary for the month of January 1918.

Army Form C. 2118.

WAR DIARY
—or—
INTELLIGENCE SUMMARY.

(Erase heading not required.)

126th Divisional Trench Mortar Batteries

Place	Date	Hour	Summary of Events and Information	Remarks and references to Appendices
HARGICOURT.	1918 1st Jan		Owing to advese weather conditions firing impossible - Personnel engaged on preparing reserve positions	
	2		do	
	3		do	
	4		do	
	5		do	
	6		do	
	7		do	
	8		do	
	9		do	
	10		do	
	11		do	
	12		Medium Batteries fired 10rds regarding K10 LANE & RUBY WOOD.	
	13		Firing impossible. Personnel employed on reserve positions	
	14		Medium Batteries fired 7Rds a phosgene working parties on BUCKSHOT RAVINE.	
	15		Medium Batteries fired 35rds at enemy wire & track at hostile T.M. at G.2.a.70.40. This T.M. was observed firing & was silenced by our 6" mortars	

Army Form C. 2118.

WAR DIARY
or
INTELLIGENCE SUMMARY.
(Erase heading not required.)

Instructions regarding War Diaries and Intelligence Summaries are contained in F. S. Regs., Part II. and the Staff Manual respectively. Title pages will be prepared in manuscript.

Place	Date	Hour	Summary of Events and Information	Remarks and references to Appendices
HARGICOURT	19.18			
	16 Jan		Medium Howitzer fired 24 rds on enemy wire at A.25.d.30.30 & G.2.c.1.4.	
	17"	do	Fired 45 rds on wire at A.25.d.15.30 & G.2.c.1.4. Wire much cut.	
			Heavy Battery fired 6 rds registering G.2.b.10.55 & 4 rds on A.26.a.16.30.	
	18"		Engaged on various positions & enemy ammunition dump.	
	19"		Medium Howitzer fired 22 rds on wire A.25.d.10.30 & G.2.c.1.4.	
			Heavy Battery fired 8 rds on DOUBLEMONT FARM.	
	20"		Howitzers fired 100 rds on wire A.25.a.10.30 & G.2.c.1.4. Wire much very heavy damage.	
	21"		Do. fired 196 rds on wire & dugouts in support of raid by RIFLE BRIGADE.	
	22"		Heavy Battery fired 12 rds. Ditto.	
	23"		Active. Heavy fired 4 rds on RUBY WOOD.	
			Medium Howitzers firing on track junction at G.1.b. Damage caused to two emplacements and	
			heavy firing then 8 rds on A.20.c.4.3 & 8 rds at G.2.b.3.6.	
			Heavy Artillery fired 14 rds on WIND TRENCH A.26.b.3.3 & 10 rds on hostile T.M. at G.2.a.10.10.	
	24"		Medium Howitzers fired 4 rds on hostile T.M. at G.1.a.8.5 & 26 rds on wire at G.1.d.85.85.	
	25"		Heavy Battery fired 16 rds on hostile T.M. at G.2.d.10.50 & 6 rds on A.20.d.45.25.	
	26"		Medium Howitzers fired 22 rds on trench & dumps at A.25.d. & G.2.d.10.7.1.35.95.	

Army Form C. 2118.

WAR DIARY
or
INTELLIGENCE SUMMARY.
(Erase heading not required.)

Instructions regarding War Diaries and Intelligence Summaries are contained in F. S. Regs., Part II. and the Staff Manual respectively. Title pages will be prepared in manuscript.

Place	Date	Hour	Summary of Events and Information	Remarks and references to Appendices
HARICOURT.	26th		Heavy Shelling found Craters on hostile T.M. at G.7.d.20.60.	
	27"		Medium Hostile found Battn in trenches at G.2.a.8.5 x G.2.c.55.10 the observer reported the enemy to meet	
	28"		" found craters on G.2.a.0.5	
			Do	
	29"		Do found craters on trenches in front of G.2.a.8.5; G.2.c.63.15 x G.7 d. 23.25	
			Heavy Shelling field Bk on hostile T.M. at G.2.b.2.6	
	30"		Medium Hostile found M. on new trenches at G.2.a.8.5 x G.7.d.80.35	
			Do found M.M. on RUBY WOOD.	
	31st		Heavy Shelling field Bk at G.2.b.1.2	

Vol 20

Confidential

War Diary
for
month of February 1918

2nd Divisional Trench Mortar Batteries

Army Form C. 2118.

WAR DIARY
—or—
INTELLIGENCE SUMMARY.

(Erase heading not required.) 9th Divisional Branch Mortar Battery

Instructions regarding War Diaries and Intelligence
Summaries are contained in F. S. Regs., Part II.
and the Staff Manual respectively. Title pages
will be prepared in manuscript.

Place	Date	Hour	Summary of Events and Information	Remarks and references to Appendices
HARGICOURT	1.2.18		Adverse weather conditions prevented firing - Personnel engaged on various positions.	
	2"		Medium Battery fired 18rds on enemy guns at G.2.a.80.50 & G.1.d 87.18 – 95.13 ft fusee splinters.	
	3"		do do 16rds on OP in trench. Hits were successfully cut.	
	4"		Heavy Bty Mng fired 9rds on A.20.c.10.25 & 9rds on G.2.b 2.6 (hostile MTPs)	
			Medium Battery fired 16 rds on wire. Completing the gaps already made.	
			Heavy Battery fired 13rds on hostile TM at G.2.b 2.6 & 12rds OUENNEMONT FARM.	
	5"		Medium Battery fired 6rds on selected targets in support of raid	
			Heavy Battery fired 6rds on M36 d.4.8	
	6"		Medium Battery fired 12rds in response to S.O.S.	
			ditto	
	7"		Heavy Battery fired 18 rds.	
	8"		Personnel engaged on various positions.	
			Heavy Bty fired 5rds on hostile MTP. at G.2.7.6.2.6 – Medium Bty successfully engaged enemy posts.	
	9"		Personnel engaged on various positions.	
	10"		Heavy Bty fired 8rds on A.20 d.02.30.	
			Medium Battery fired 8rds on SOS lines in response to S.O.S	
	11"		Heavy Battery fired 13rds. ditto.	

Army Form C. 2118.

WAR DIARY
or
INTELLIGENCE SUMMARY.
(Erase heading not required.)

Instructions regarding War Diaries and Intelligence Summaries are contained in F. S. Regs., Part II. and the Staff Manual respectively. Title pages will be prepared in manuscript.

Place	Date	Hour	Summary of Events and Information	Remarks and references to Appendices
HARICOURT	12th		Medium Balloon fired 22nd regarding T.T. KID EDGE LANES by aeroplane	
	13th		Heavy Batty fired 1 rd. on enemy defences Trench T.T. position	
	14th		Heavy Batty fired 2 rd. on A.26 d.30.80	
	15th		Personal engaged on trench positions	
	16th		Heavy Batty fired 10 rds. on G.3 d.7.6 + A.26 d.4.8	
	17th		do 10 rds on A.26 a 90.60 – 93.05	
	18th		Personnel employed on trench positions	
	19th		do	
	20th		Heavy Batter fired 5 rds. on Hostile MTM at G.2.L.2.6.	
	21st		Medium Batterie fired 8 rds regarding RUBY WOOD	
			do fired 120 rds on TRUBY WOOD.	
	22nd		Heavy Batty fired 10 rds on A.26 a 99.20 + G.2.6.2.6	
	23rd		Heavy Batty fired 6 rds on G.2.L.2.6	
			Personnel engaged on trench positions	
	24th		Heavy Batty fired 2 rds on hostile defences + Trench position	
	25th		Medium Batterie fired 21 rds on T.T.G.2 & T.3.7.5	

Army Form C. 2118.

WAR DIARY
or
INTELLIGENCE SUMMARY.
(Erase heading not required.)

Instructions regarding War Diaries and Intelligence Summaries are contained in F. S. Regs., Part II. and the Staff Manual respectively. Title pages will be prepared in manuscript.

Place	Date	Hour	Summary of Events and Information	Remarks and references to Appendices
HARBOURT	25th		Heavy Shrapnel fire on A 26 a 9.3 05	
	26		Several incidents on positions	
	27		Whizz Bang fired 8 rds on G.14 a & G 2 c 10.20	
	28		Medium Bohrs fired 80 rds on S.O.S lines in response to S.O.S. Heavy Batty fired 9 rds on S.O.S lines + 22 rds on hostile battery	
	Note		During the month of February the Heart Mortar Batteries encompassing the Heavy help on new lose people and the Medium Batteries consist of 4 x 6 other 4 pdr's being amalgamated with X+Y	
			The T.O.A. personnel of the Medium Batteries have been transferred to the Heavy Batts.	

D J Monro

Capt RA
a/Adjt No 20 DA

2353 Wt W2544/1454 700,000 5/15 D. D. & L. A.D.S.S./Forms/C. 2118.

Army Form C. 2118.

WAR DIARY
or
INTELLIGENCE SUMMARY.
(Erase heading not required.)

4th Divisional 4th Batteries

Va 21

Place	Date	Hour	Summary of Events and Information	Remarks and references to Appendices
HARGICOURT	1918 1st		Engaged on warm positions	
	2		do	
	3		Fired 40 rds on enemy approach in response to S.O.S.	
	4		70 rds in organized bombardment on enemy Line emplacements	
	5		Relieved by 66th T.M.Bn. and proceeded to BEAUMETZ	
BEAUMETZ	6		In reserve to cavalry corps – Training	
	7		do	
	8		do	
	9		do	
	10		do	
	11		do	
	12		do	
LE VERGUIER	13		Relieved cavalry corps T.M. in line	
	14		Personnel employed on positions	
	15		do	
	16		do	

Army Form C. 2118.

WAR DIARY
or
INTELLIGENCE SUMMARY.
(Erase heading not required.)

Instructions regarding War Diaries and Intelligence Summaries are contained in F. S. Regs., Part II. and the Staff Manual respectively. Title pages will be prepared in manuscript.

Place	Date	Hour	Summary of Events and Information	Remarks and references to Appendices
LE VERGUIER	17th		Engaged on works boundaries	
	18		do	
	19		do	
	20		do	
	21st	1–2 am	Fired 55.3 do on enemy in RED LINE & FLEMING CRATER.	
		4–39	5 rds on MAREVAL TRENCH during enemy attack on VADENCOURT.	
		10.30 am	100 rds on lost hands on notley N.W. of VADENCOURT.	
		3.30 am 22nd	Established and maintained two forward dumps at LIHONS &	
	25th		do. evening established dump at HARBONIÈRE	
	26th		do	
	27th		To takes of dumps between HARBONIÈRE & CAIX.	
	28th		do	
	29th		on the SAINS – COTTENCHY ROAD.	
	30th		Collard 15 men to A.R.P.	

Signed / ?
O/C Coy 2h? ?

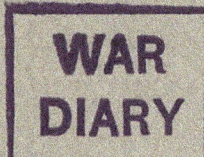

24th DIVISIONAL TRENCH MORTAR BATTERIES.

A P R I L

1 9 1 8

24th Divisional T.M. Batteries

Confidential

War Diary for month of April 1918.

INTELLIGENCE SUMMARY.

(Erase heading not required.)

2nd Divisional French Mortar Batteries

Place	Date	Hour	Summary of Events and Information	Remarks and references to Appendices
RUMIGNY	1918 April 1st		Awaiting Orders to take over Ammunition Dumps at COTTENCHY 68 O.R. attached 2nd D.A.C.	
	2nd		ditto	
	3rd		Proceeded to COTTENCHY and took over Dumps. 1 Officer & 8 O.R. formed & maintained Dump at S. NICHOLAS	
COTTENCHY	4th		At COTTENCHY DUMP.	
	5th		do	
	6th		do	
	7th		do	
	8th		Moved SALOUEL and left same evening to take charge of DURY DUMP.	
SALOUEL	9th		At DURY DUMP.	
DURY	10th		Moved CLAIRY	
CLAIRY	11th		" ANDAINVILLE	
ANDAINVILLE	12th		Left ANDAINVILLE and proceeded to WANEL	
	13th		At WANEL Interior Training	
WANEL	14th		do " "	
	15th		do " "	
	16th		Personnel reported from D.A.C.	

INTELLIGENCE SUMMARY.

(Erase heading not required.)

Place	Date	Hour	Summary of Events and Information	Remarks and references to Appendices
WANEL	1918 April 17th		Left WANEL & proceeded to NEUF-MOULIN - Car proceeded to A.S.C.	
WAVANS	18th		Arrived WAVANS	
RAMECOURT	19th		H RAMECOURT & Training	
	20th		ditto	
	21st		Left RAMECOURT & proceeded to BERLENCOURT	
BERLENCOURT	22nd		Training	
	23rd		do	
	24th		do	
	25th		do	
	26th		do	
	27th		do	
	28th		do	
	29th		do	
	30th		do	

Capt/RFA
D.T.M.Q. 2nd D.A.
30/4/18

WD 23

24th. Divisional Trench Mortar Batteries

Confidential

War Diary for the month of May 1918.

Army Form C. 2118.

WAR DIARY
—or—
INTELLIGENCE SUMMARY.

(Erase heading not required.)

24th Divisional Trench Mortar Battery

Place	Date	Hour	Summary of Events and Information	Remarks and references to Appendices
BERLENCOURT	1918 1 May		Snowing	
	2 "		ditto	
LENS.	3 "		Relieved 3rd Canadian Res T.M. Battery	
	4 "		Fired 40 rds harassing fire during night on suspected movement	
	5 "		Firing nil	
	6 "		Firing nil	
	7 "		Around shoot carried out of 4/XIII M.T.M.B.	
	8 "		Fired 111 rds on N.9.a + N.9.c on retaliation for hostile T.M.	
	9 "		Fired 30 rds on trench junctions on H.20.c + H.26.a also on hostile T.M. emplacements	
	10 "		Fired 125 rds on enemy defences & M.G. positions on N.9.a + c, N.14.b.8. & H.26.c	
	11 "		Fired 66 rds on defences on N.3.c, N.14.b & H.26.b - Good results obtained.	
	12 "		Fired 100 rds on trench junctions & minnenwerfer bands on H.26.b + H.32.b + N.14.a+c	
	13 "		Fired 113 rounds 9 T.M. + N.3c N.9a + N.14.a.b. in retaliation from hostile T.M.	
	13 "		Fired 121 rds on trench bonds N.14.a+c N.8.b + H.26.a+c - Rocket dumps exploded	
			an enemy large d. machine gun blown out of trench	
	14 "		Fired 17 rds on Coy HQ, N.14.c + Sensitive Points in N.14.a.b. + H.26.a+c.	
	15 "		Fired 108 rds on junction of LENS - LaBASSEE + LENS-BETHUNE Rds - Good results obtained	

Army Form C. 2118.

WAR DIARY
or
INTELLIGENCE SUMMARY.

(Erase heading not required.)

Instructions regarding War Diaries and Intelligence Summaries are contained in F.S. Regs., Part II. and the Staff Manual respectively. Title pages will be prepared in manuscript.

Place	Date	Hour	Summary of Events and Information	Remarks and references to Appendices
	1915			
	16 May		Recd. 18 rnds on enemy TMs in N.3.c - H.33.c & H.26.d - Direct shoot on tackle the	
	17th		MGs on enemy dugouts & TM emplacements	
	18th		68 rds on hostile posts in N.W.c - N.9.a.c & M.G. at H.32.c.15.25.	
	19th		12 rnds on enemy TMs at N.9.c & N.3.c & H.26.a.6. Good work observed	
	20th		13 rnds on enemy TM, T.T. remains found 150x n Hole front.	
	21st		14 " on enemy MW N.W.a.90.60. H.26.d.15.10 & 7M " N.9.c.	
	22nd		230 " Enemy work defences & TM positions upon white front. Excellent work obtained	
	23rd		336 " On enemy NW a 80 bo. en fortification for road also in wire at H.26 d.15.10	
			N 32 d. w.G 80 & H.32 d. 70.50. Good work in area of woodplace	
	24th		110 rds Concrete at N.W.a.80.60. H.26 d.15-10 H.32.d.H.080 & H.32.d. 70.50.	
	25th		238 rds On Cross Roads and Railway N.W.C. Coys H.Q. T.Ks & M.G.s in N.6.a.w	
			Conjunction with raid by R WEST KENTS, for which more had been successfully cut	
			140 rds Enemy TMs & snipers posts in N.3.c - N.W.t. & also on wire H.32 d.25.	
	26th		H.26.d.- During one of our shoots on this day a premature occurred	
			on N° 3 gun of 170 TMB fatally destroying gun & wounding N°1	
			and retaliation to our fire the enemy opened out a few bombardment	

Army Form C. 2118.

WAR DIARY
or
INTELLIGENCE SUMMARY.

(Erase heading not required.)

Instructions regarding War Diaries and Intelligence Summaries are contained in F. S. Regs., Part II. and the Staff Manual respectively. Title pages will be prepared in manuscript.

Place	Date	Hour	Summary of Events and Information	Remarks and references to Appendices
			on the positions of Htely. No H gun received a direct hit which turned the gun and caused 6 casualties to personnel. No 5 position was rendered unapproachable owing to the entrance being blown in.	
	27th		Fired 170 rds on enemy TMs & TJs in N.9. N.3.c. N.md. H.32.d. & H.33.c.	
	28th		" 101 rds on Coy H.Q. TMs & TJs N.9.c & N.14.c also whose were H.32.b. 30.90 & H.32.b.2.c.	
	29th		" 161 " on counter-attack upon our rifle front & upon guns at H.32.b. 3.9	
	30th		" 90 " on TMs & TJs & defensive fronts N.9 & N.3.c. & 26 a & H.32.b.	
	31st		" 155 " on MebdN.9.d.20.70 & TMs in N.3.c, H.26.d.10.80, H.32.b.6050-90.70	

Capt RFA
D.T.O. 20Dh
31/5/18

2353 Wt.W25414454 700,000 5/15 D.D.&L. A.D.S.S./Forms/C. 2118.

Vol 24

Confidential

War Diary

of

Divisional Trench Mortar Officer 24th Div. Artillery.

From 1st June 1918

To 30th June 1918.

Army Form C. 2118.

WAR DIARY or INTELLIGENCE SUMMARY.

(Erase heading not required.)

Instructions regarding War Diaries and Intelligence Summaries are contained in F.S. Regs., Part II. and the Staff Manual respectively. Title pages will be prepared in manuscript.

Place	Date	Hour	Summary of Events and Information	Remarks and references to Appendices
Field	June			
	1.		Fired 31 rds. 9 successfully cut wire at N8d x7. 20 fired on T/S Hq a 9a H32b	
	2.		50 rds on enemy TM8 HQ J7.3. 20 rds fired on Offensive.	
	3.		Fired 60 rds successfully cutting wire, & distinct gaps being made.	
	4.		Registered 9 neutralised enemy TMs 9 pull-down barrage in support of raid.	
	5.		100 rds fired on enemy TMB 9 HQ.	
	6.		Wire cutting & silencing enemy TMs 53 rds fired at T.J. H32.b.6.1 in support of raid.	
	7.		Since 160 rds 9 cut wire at H8.b N2.d 9 replied strongly to enemy TM fire.	
	8.		144 rds wire expended in support of raid	
	9.		80 rds. Offensive fired	
	10.		30 rds in retaliation on enemy TMs 9 support line.	
	11.		Hostile TMs kept quiet by strong counter TM fire 106 rds fired.	
	12.		161 rds on enemy front line 9 TMS.	
	13.		Enemies TM shoots 68 rds in support of fighting patrol of RWK	
	14.		83 rds wire cutting 9 retaliation	
	15.		49 rds on enemy wire at H2 a 7.3 2 Coy HQ 9 TMs.	
	16.		Expended 56 rds on wire cut H2 d 7.3 9 hostile T.M.S.	

Army Form C. 2118.

WAR DIARY
or
INTELLIGENCE SUMMARY.
(Erase heading not required.)

Instructions regarding War Diaries and Intelligence Summaries are contained in F. S. Regs., Part II. and the Staff Manual respectively. Title pages will be prepared in manuscript.

Place	Date	Hour	Summary of Events and Information	Remarks and references to Appendices
Ficheux	June 17		32 yds lifted on counted TM work & wire cutting.	
	18		80 rds Retaliation. 80 rds in support of raid by 73rd I.B.	
	19		4½ rds Retaliation on HQ & TMs. 8½ rds wire cutting at No-d 68.99.	
	20		14 rds wire cutting at NORMAN STACKS N¾ 3.24. also engaged enemy T.M.B.	
	21		3 rds registration. 45 rds on enemy front line in H96 d 3.H32 b.	
	22		14 rds on NORMAN STACKS N¾ 2. 68.99.	
	23		34 rds Retaliation on enemy TMs 9TT. 60 rds Offensive.	
	24		13 rds wire cutting NORMAN STACKS. 61 rds Retaliation on enemy TMs.	
	25		118 yds M.G. & I wire cutting NORMAN STACKS.	
	26		158 rds in Retaliation on enemy TMs & HQ	
	27		180 rds wire cutting at N9d 95.14 9N8 2.8.5. 70 rds Offensive.	
	28		120 rds in support of raid & 30 rds hostile TMs.	
	29		78 yds hostile TMs & wire cutting 70 rds on enemy trenches. Offensive.	
	30		20 rds wire cutting & 110 retaliation D Offensive.	

2353 Wt. W2544/1454 700,000 5/15 D. D. & L. A.D.S.S./Forms/C. 2118.

CONFIDENTIAL

WAR DIARY

of

24th. DIVISIONAL TRENCH MORTAR OFFICER.

From 1st JULY, 1918.   To 31st JULY, 1918.

Original
DTMO
WAR DIARY 2 Div
or
INTELLIGENCE SUMMARY.
(Erase heading not required.)

Army Form C. 2118.

July 1915

Place	Date July	Hour	Summary of Events and Information	Remarks and references to Appendices
Juilet.	1	3.30	55 Rds. fired at Enemy Divn. The following targets were also engaged T.J. N.9.C. 40. 95. N.A.86.B.	
"	2	2.00	Bombarded 169 Rds. 41 on Enemy Divn. N.2.d.6.4.9. N.3.c.0.4. (Retaliation on Enemy Trenches) B.14, H.26. 9.H.33.	
"	3	3.00	125 Rds. on Enemy Divn. T.J. and T.M.S.	
"	4		325 Rds fired at Enemy Divn. T.M's 15.9.16 in N.8 were heavily bombarded, also numerous T.J.	
"	5		175 Rds on T.M's. H.A.9. Trenches in retaliation also H.26. a.b.c.	
"	6	130	Rds " at Various Targets. Proceeding 06.14.15. M.G. H.26. N.3. and M.g.	
"	7	200	" on Enemy Front & Support Trenches Post at F.8.b.89.65. T.M. F.8.14. F.9.	
"	8	190	" on Various Targets. Dugouts 14.a.64.95. T.M. F.D. 14. N.9 and Trenches	
"	9	130	" " Post N.9. b.69.93. and Trenches H.32.7 36. also Divn.	
"	10	167	" Trenches " 12.33. T.M. H. 26.a.8.5. Post N.8.d.8".85". Nottes T.M".	
"	11	186	" on Southern of Road Ly.M. 1.8. also Trenches H.26.c. 9.32.d. T.M". N.9.a. Nos.9.F.	
"	12	141	" on Post N.8.b.81.65. Retaliation T.M. N.9.a.24.93. S.T. N.14.b. 50.66.	
"	13	152	" " N.F.d.64.85. Trenches in H.26. and 32. barricade front on	
"	14	174	" Carried out offensive shoots on Post N.8.6.81.85. also trenches H.26.c. & and.	
"	15	192	" Bombarded " in offensive & retaliation shoots. The posts in N.8.b.69.65. T.M". N.9. N.14 Shelters	
"	16	180	" Shoots on Enemy Posts T.J. T.M. in N.9.a.2. H.3.c. & N.y. barricades	
"	17	200	" Continued and Existing at H.32.d.15.90. H.Q. T.M? T.J. N.9.a.9 N.3.c.	
"	18	180	" Shoots on NUDGE, NEGRO, NARROW Trenches also Shortz T.M".	

Army Form C. 2118.

WAR DIARY
or
INTELLIGENCE SUMMARY.

(Erase heading not required.)

Instructions regarding War Diaries and Intelligence Summaries are contained in F.S. Regs., Part II. and the Staff Manual respectively. Title pages will be prepared in manuscript.

continued

Place	Date	Hour	Summary of Events and Information	Remarks and references to Appendices
Field	July 19	14.5	Col. Grapendell on leave. Cutting at H.32.d.4.4.; also fired on T.M. 15, N.9, No. 15, 16 & 12 N.3.	
"	20	20.0	" Offensive shoots on enemy guns on NUDGE & NARROW, T.M. 15 & 16 N.3. also line N.32.d.	
"	21	18.7	" " " " N.9. H.32.d. H.32.c.d.	
"	22	17.0	" on hostile T.M.'s q in support of Raid H.32.d.50.50., N.9.4. 70.70.	
"	23	15.0	" Post N.3.d.8.7. Fetched. N.F.6. Y.N.3.d., 9 lunches on H.26.32.9.33.	
"	24	342	" Supported Raids by 14/S.and 43rd Inf. Bdes. also Headquarters H.26.9.32.	
"	25	101	" Retaliated on T.J.7.N.3.e. & T.M. N.6.14.N.9.a. Offensive burst on H.26.9.22.	
"	26	199	" On Gun durn at N.8.b. 80.95, 9 NORMAN STACKS. Wirecuts on H.21.9.33.	
"	27	91	" On trenches N.26.9 N.14.	
"	28	223	" Burst on guns and Munr H.32.b.45.90. Movement at N.8.b.89.88 & Retaliation	
"	29	180	" Extended in Retaliation for Enemy shelling 9 T.M. 16. N.3.; also were in H.32.d.7d.	
"	30	199	" on Enemy T.M. H.Q. & T.J. Offensive shoots on H.32.d.& H.32.d.	
"	31	341	" Were H.32.d. & H.32.d. in support of raid by 9th E.Lanc. Regt.	

During month tuck several reinforcements.

[signature]
Capt. R.F.A.
D.T.M.O. 34th D.A.

7/8/18.

CONFIDENTIAL.

WAR DIARY.

OF

Divisional Trench Mortar Officer.(24th Division).

From:- 1st August 1918.   To:- 30th August 1918.

24th Divisional T.M. Batteries.

Army Form C. 2118.

WAR DIARY
or
INTELLIGENCE SUMMARY.
(Erase heading not required.)

Instructions regarding War Diaries and Intelligence Summaries are contained in F. S. Regs., Part II. and the Staff Manual respectively. Title pages will be prepared in manuscript.

Place	Date	Hour	Summary of Events and Information	Remarks and references to Appendices
Field	August 1		193 Rounds Expended on retaliation in support of raid & Enemy Wire H.32.b & d	
	2		105 " Offensive and retaliation shoots. Wire H.32.b & H.32.d	
	3		146 " Enemy Wire H.32.b & H.32.d & Retaliation for hostile T.M.	
	4		148 " On Enemy Wire H.32.b & d. X/34 wirecutting as ordered	
	5		120 " Wirecutting rinefly H.32.b & d. N.8.a.13.05, N.9.a.23.80, N.14c.65.94, also H.32.b & d	
	6		146 " N.8.d.16.28, N.9.9.21.41, N.9.a.24.28, also hostile M.G. & T.M.	
	7		150 " N.8.d.30.52, N.8.L.80.95. N.8.L.95.40, T.M. N.2.d 3.g.np Questions	
	8		116 " N.9.a.24.28, N.14c.65.94, T.M. H.26.a 80.50, T.J. H.26.d 15.30, H.26 c 31.09	
	9		119 " N.9.a.24.28 H.26 d 98.65. H.26 c 85.10 offensive	
	10		117 " N.2.d 95.11. N.9.a.24.28. H.26 d 98.65. H.26 c 85.10 offensive	
	11		131 " N.2.d 75.90, 80q. N.9.a 2.75 Retl H.26.a 02.97. H.26.a 95.35 offensive	
	12		127 " T.M. N.9.a 93.80 M.G post N.14a 70.30. Offensive H26 a 96.65. H26.d 95.65	
	13		153 " T.M. N.9.a 24.28, 23.80, 7.3. N.9.a 21.41. M.G post. N.14.a 70.30, H26.d 15.90 Offensive	
	14		90 " M.G. Emplaced. N.14.a.30.90. spit. N.14c 10.95. sniper at N.14.a 99.70 H26 a 64 ou "	
	15		137 " Working Porty N.14.a 65.50. T.M. N.3.c 75.40 Enemy post N.8.L 86.90 H 26 d 15.30 "	
	16		130 " N.14.a 6.6 T.M. N.9a 28 wire H.32.2. 9.H.32.L.	

2353 Wt W2541/1454 700,000 5/15 D. D. & L. A.D.S.S./Forms/C. 2118.

Army Form C. 2118.

WAR DIARY
or
INTELLIGENCE SUMMARY.
(Erase heading not required.)

Instructions regarding War Diaries and Intelligence Summaries are contained in F. S. Regs. Part II. and the Staff Manual respectively. Title pages will be prepared in manuscript.

Place	Date	Hour	Summary of Events and Information	Remarks and references to Appendices
Field	August 17		130 rds expended on Pill Box N17a 6.5, TM N9a 25.80. H28a 75.60. H28a 75.60. H32d. H32d.	Offensive.
	18		160 " N17a 6.5, TM N9a 25.60 wire H32d. 94/32d.	
	19		135 " " N17a 6.5. TM N9a 25.80. wire H32d. H38c. H96 05.35	Offensive
	20		116 " " N17a 6.5 TM N9a 95.80 arc N8b 85.95 Right Coolie Pt/dugouts H25 & 10.7)	
	21		160 " " wire N8b 86.95. Trench N9a 98.96. H96 & 05.96. H96 & 14.96	Offensive
	22		90 " " TMs. N3c 22 38. N9a 94 28-25.80. 9. H96 & 57 65-75. H96a 89.50	Offensive
	23		130 " " N3c 22 38. CT N14b 95.35 Coy HQ. N14c 20.16 H32 & 83. H32d 25.66 "	
	24		217 " " N9a 24 98. Enemy post N14b 65.80 CT N14b 76.35 TM N9a 93.50 H96 & 3.2. H96 & 6.6	
	25		177 " " N3a 22 38 HQ. N14c 30.46 & CT N9a 0605. H96 & 3.1. H2 00.9 H96 & 2.0	
	26		137 " " wire N8d 31.46. N14a 60.90 TM & H32 & 73.28 H32 & 00 82	
	27		138 " " " N14a 80.00 H96central 0) H96a 66.05 H52 & 95.95	
	28		134 " " wire N8d 15.08 TM N9a 97.93. H96 & 0895. H96 & 95.65 H33a 0585	Offensive
	29		187 " " N8d 10.95. N14 & 49.69. N9a 30.23. N14c 22.95. N9c 50.89. H32 & 95.20. H32 & 42-28	
	30		266 " " N3e. M.G. N.S. a TM Eng. N9.e. Tel N14.6.33. TM 15/16. N3e. 20.40. N.20 & 40.80. N. 20 app: 10	
	31		50 " " T. J. N.3.e. TM No. 15 N3e T.M. 15 I Dugouts N.20.a.8.8.	
	1st September 1918.			

Capt RFA
D.T.M.O. 24" D.A.

WAR DIARY or INTELLIGENCE SUMMARY

Army Form C. 2118.

24 T.M.B.

Place	Date	Hour	Summary of Events and Information	Remarks and references to Appendices
Field	Sept	1	127. Rounds Expended on Wire N.3.e, N.9.e, Harrasing fire Byroad on N.9.e.30.90, N.20.a.85.90. Suspected M.G.	
		2	30. " Offensive Shoots N.9.a.45.92 + N.3.e.30.13.	
		3	64. " Wire N.3.e.00.20 to N.3.e.00.40. T LENS STATION.	
		4	123. " N.3.e.10.40 + N.3.e.10.00. Harassing fire on N.9.e.00.40 + N.9.e.40.	
		5	133. " N.2.d.90.90. T.J. N.3.e.05.30. R.P. N.2.d.05.95. T.J. N.3.e.05.30. N.20.2.3.3 (also Retaliatory Shoot)	
		6	123. " N.2.a.98.20 + N.2.d.90.40. M.G's N.3.e.15.50 + N.3.e.20.10 + N.20.b.50.35	
		7	105. " Directing N.3.e.08.06, N.3.e.08.15, N.9.a.05.95. Shell Hole N.3.e.30.10. N.20.b.34 + N.20.a.6.6	
		8	166. " N.2.d.65.95, N.3.e.05.10, N.3.e.10.05 (M.G). N.9.e.10.50, Wire N.20.b.5.5	
		9	169. " Offensive Shoot on N.2.a.70.65, N.8.b.90.52, N.8.b.90.60, M.G. N.8.d.30.35, N.9.a.7.1) N.20.b.8.5	
		10	154. " Wire in support of raid N.3.e.05.85 + N.8.b.92.95 Offensive Shoot T. N.2.d.92.61 N.20.a.6	
		11	100. " Directing H.8 b.74.14.90.45. Wire damaged at N.8.b.90.40 + N.8.b.95.90	
		12	204. " N.9.a.09.93. Wire damaged at N.9.a.16.40 N.14.92.40 + N.9.a.10.40	
		13	296. " N.9.a.06.05 to N.8.6.23.18. N.14.a.99.12, H.32.d.40.40 to H.32.d.40.60	
		14	310. " N.K.t.80.40. N.r.t.90.40 N.8.d.05.00, N.14.6.20.20, H.32.d.40.40 to H.32.d.40	
		15	290. " N.8.6.40.00 to N.8.b.40.30, N.8.d. H.32.d. 40.10 to N.2.b.65.40.	
		16	149. " N.9.a.09.99), N.2.6.60.60. N.2.b.40.95, H.32.a.85.10 to H.32.a.99.00	

WAR DIARY or INTELLIGENCE SUMMARY

Army Form C. 2118.

Continued

Place	Date	Hour	Summary of Events and Information	Remarks and references to Appendices
Field	Sept	17	203 rounds expended on Wiring etc. at N.8.d.09.00; N.g.a.95.45; N.2.d; N.3.e.00.90; H.32.d.90.10; N.24.65.40	
		18	197 "	N.3.c.05.40; N.8.d.70.20; N.g.e.90.10; N.2.t.65.80 to H.32.d.95.20.
		19	184 "	N.g.e.08.50. N.8.o.d.80.10 to N.15.a.35.40, & H.32.d.95.20.
		20	146 "	N.2.d.70.80; N.g.e.20.50; N.g.e.25.80; N.g.c.50.20, & H.32.d.
		21	207 "	N.2.d.60.80; N.g.a.20.30; N.8.l.60.60 & H.32.d.
		22	171 "	N.g.a.30.50; N.g.a.20.55; N.g.c, & H.32.d.90.10 to H.32.d.99.55.
		23	131 "	N.8.d.46.69; N.8.d.56; N.6.d.35.52. H.32.d
		24	216 "	Offensive shoots on N.g.a.20.45; J.1.N.8.c.94.40; N.g.e.20.55, also H.32.d.
		25	269 "	MG " T.J. N.8.d.55.30. M.6.N.g.c.10.45 also N.2.6.95.95
		26	1584 "	in support of Raid N.8.d.9 & N.g.c.05.30 & selected targets by Heavy Artillery (H. Coy reserved)
		27	93 "	M.G. & 99.15; N.8.& 99.90. N1.40.40. N.g.a.15.50. Y.9.d.99.90
		28	105 "	T.M. N.g.c.00.50. Dugout N.4.d.10.05; J.N.8.t.90.90. Y.4.33.& 20.80.
		29	120 "	S.O.S fired at N.4.d.10.25; N.4.d.90.60; N.g.c.40.25; N.3.c.35.10 & T.d.M.2.k.77.10
		30	116 "	Nuns Alley N.g.e.65.50; N.3.e.35.40. LT.M. N.3.a.40.40.

1st October 1916.

H. Haynes Capt. RFA
A/D.T.M.O. 24th D.A.

MC In Bt Vol 28

WAR DIARY
or
INTELLIGENCE SUMMARY.
(Erase heading not required.)

Army Form C. 2118.

Instructions regarding War Diaries and Intelligence Summaries are contained in F. S. Regs., Part II. and the Staff Manual respectively. Title pages will be prepared in manuscript.

Place	Date	Hour	Summary of Events and Information	Remarks and references to Appendices
Field	Oct 1		116 Rounds Expended on Offensive Shoots at N.9.c.65.50; N.3.c.35.40; N.3.a.40.40	
	2		152 " " " N.9.c.28.38; N.8.6.92.90; N.9.c.20.20; N.8.d.90.65	
	3		No firing possible owing to enemy withdrawal	
	4		20 Rounds Expended on Offensive Shoot on N.16.t.90.00; N.16.L.90.20	
	5		27 " " " N.11.d.5.65; N.11.L N.12.a.90.50; N.11.a.	
	6		16 " " "	
	7		20 " " " M.C. N.12.c.90.45	
	8		40 " " " N.12.a.40; N.9.a.5.4	
	9		50 " " " N.11.6.3.4; N.11.d.90.85; 4.36.a.40.	
	10		32 " " " N.6.t.65.10; N.11.d.65.85; N.6.A. Central. N.6.c.23	
	11		40 " " " N.11.t.40.85; Main H.36.a.	
	12		No firing H.36.a. Wirecutting	
	13		2nd Div 1.M Batteries relieved by 58th Div 1.M.B.	
	14		Rested at Wagon Lines Bully Grenay	
	15		Proceeded by Motor lorries to GUEMAPPE	
	16		CAMBRAI.	

WAR DIARY
or
INTELLIGENCE SUMMARY

Army Form C. 2118.

Place	Date	Hour	Summary of Events and Information	Remarks and references to Appendices
RUES	6/11		Refitting & Training at CAMBRAI.	
	18		Intended by Motor Lorry to AVESNES LES AUBERT	
	19		2 6" Mobile T.M's in action at MONTRECOURT	
	20		Mired forward with Infantry to Farm CARONNE, WEST OF SOMMAING	
	21		45 rounds fired on strong point on road junction SOMMAING	
	22		35 " M.G. Near SOMMAING	
	23		40 " M.G. Y.R.M.?	
	24		Subscribed to 61st Divn attack with 2 6" T.M's fired at hostile M.G.'s holding up advance at VENDREIES	
	25		6" Mobile T.M's advanced with Infantry West of ARTRES.	
	26		1 " placed in action at ARTRES. Fired 20 rds at hostile M.G."	
	27		No firing possible owing to rapid advance by Infantry	
	28		1 Mobile T.M. fired at Strong point East of SEPMERIES	
	29		60 rounds fired at road West of ARTRES on LA PAUVRET	
	30		20 " " hostile M.G.'s holding up advance	
	31		18 " " at request of Bath. Commander	

15-11-18

W Mansel Capt. R.F.A.
A/DTM.O 5Y DD A

Army Form C. 2118

24 D TM By

9/R 29

WAR DIARY
INTELLIGENCE SUMMARY.
(Erase heading not required.)

Instructions regarding War Diaries and Intelligence Summaries are contained in F. S. Regs., Part II. and the Staff Manual respectively. Title pages will be prepared in manuscript.

Place	Date	Hour	Summary of Events and Information	Remarks and references to Appendices
Field	Nov 1			
	2		2 Mobile T.M's in action at MARESCHES, supporting 61st Divn Infantry	
	3		Nothing to Report	
	4		2 Mobile T.M's in support of 73rd Inf Bde, fired 50 rds at Enemy M.G's, S.W of WAGNIES-LE-GRAND	
	5		" " action at JENLAIN	
	6		" " fired at request of 14th Inf Bde upon M.G's situated in Railway Cutting S.T. WAAST.	
	7		" " in support " " advanced towards BAVAY	
	8		Advanced with Infantry to LE CROSHENEY in the evening two T.M's were placed in action at LA BERLIERE	
	9		" to LA CRISOELLE	
	10		Nothing to Report	
	11		T.M.H.Q. removed to LA-BERLIERE	
	12		AT LA-BERLIERE	
	13		do	
	14		do	
	15		do	
	16		do	

Army Form C. 2118.

WAR DIARY
of
INTELLIGENCE SUMMARY.
(Erase heading not required.)

Instructions regarding War Diaries and Intelligence
Summaries are contained in F. S. Regs., Part II.
and the Staff Manual respectively. Title pages
will be prepared in manuscript.

Place	Date	Hour	Summary of Events and Information	Remarks and references to Appendices
Field	17		Marched to ETH	
	18		" " ESCAUDAIN	
	19		" " LEWARDE	
	20		at LEWARDE	
	21		do	
	22		do	
	23		do	
	24		do	
	25		do	
	26		do	
	27		Marched to LANDAS	
	28		at LANDAS	
	29		" "	
	30		" "	

11-12-18

6/ Mann Capt. RFA
DTMO 24th DA

Army Form C. 2118.

2nd TM 84

Vol 30

WAR DIARY
or
INTELLIGENCE SUMMARY.

(Erase heading not required.)

Instructions regarding War Diaries and Intelligence Summaries are contained in F. S. Regs., Part II. and the Staff Manual respectively. Title pages will be prepared in manuscript.

Place	Date	Hour	Summary of Events and Information	Remarks and references to Appendices
Field	Dec 1918		A. Londas	
	1			
	2			
	3			
	4			
	5			
	6			
	7			
	8			
	9			
	10			
	11			
	12			
	13			
	14			
	15			
	16			

Continued

Army Form C. 2118.

WAR DIARY
or
INTELLIGENCE SUMMARY.
(Erase heading not required.)

Instructions regarding War Diaries and Intelligence
Summaries are contained in F. S. Regs., Part II.
and the Staff Manual respectively. Title pages
will be prepared in manuscript.

Place	Date	Hour	Summary of Events and Information	Remarks and references to Appendices
Field	Dec 1918			
	17		At Landas	
	18		Marched to Cherq	
	19		At Cherq	
	20		" "	
	21		" "	
	22		" "	
	23		" "	
	24		" "	
	25		" "	
	26		" "	
	27		" "	
	28		" "	
	29		" "	
	30		" "	
	31		" "	

DS/76   JMamen Capt RFA
                                         DTMO 24th DA

Army Form C. 2118.

24 16/2

WAR DIARY
or
INTELLIGENCE SUMMARY.

(Erase heading not required.) 24th Divisional French Mortar Batteries

9 R 31

Place	Date	Hour	Summary of Events and Information	Remarks and references to Appendices
CHERCQ	1/1/19 to 31/1/19		Location P.31.d 10.00. Supplying necessary fatigue parties during these dates.	

W.H...
Capt RFA
D.T.M.O. 24th D.A.